the manager's
EMPLOYEE
ENGAGEMENT
Toolbox

Peter R. Garber

ASTD
PRESS

ASTD Press is an internationally renowned source of insightful and practical information on workplace learning, training, and professional development.

ASTD Press
1640 King Street Box 1443
Alexandria, VA 22313-1443 USA

Ordering information: Books published by ASTD Press can be purchased by visiting ASTD's website at store.astd.org or by calling 800.628.2783 or 703.683.8100.

Library of Congress Control Number: 2013951483
ISBN-10: 1-56286-860-8
ISNB-13: 978-1-56286-860-4
e-ISBN: 978-1-60728-646-2

ASTD Press Editorial Staff:
Director: Glenn Saltzman
Manager, ASTD Press: Ashley McDonald
Community Manager, Workforce Development: Ron Lippock
Senior Associate Editor: Heidi Smith
Editorial Assistant: Ashley Slade
Text and Cover Design: Lon Levy
Printed by: Versa Press, East Peoria, IL, www.versapress.com

TABLE OF CONTENTS

INTRODUCTION

EMPLOYEE ENGAGEMENT MAKES EVERYTHING BETTER

Employee engagement can sound like a very desirable concept to introduce into your workplace. But what does it really mean to be a *leader* of employee engagement, and what exactly are its benefits? This book is designed to help leaders, managers, and supervisors understand how becoming a more engaged leader can help them perform their jobs. The book will describe "What's in it for me?" about becoming a more engaged leader. And it will explain the real *advantages* for a supervisor or manager in creating a more engaged workplace for their employees.

Employee engagement really does begin with leadership. True to its name, employee engagement is about fully utilizing the talents, skills, creativity, and experiences of employees who work for you. Supervisors and managers who take advantage of employee engagement are using their most valuable resource—their employees—to reach their greatest potential. Supervisors and managers around the world have enjoyed the results of the many potential benefits of employee engagement. However, it is also important to realize that achieving your employee engagement goals doesn't happen overnight. It is a journey, just like any other challenging goal or objective you may strive to reach.

Important to understanding what employee engagement is all about is the concept of *discretionary effort*. Engaged employees give more effort, are more concerned about their jobs, and are more emotionally invested in contributing as a member of the organization. Engaged employees do more than just show up for work; they bring their hearts and their minds to their jobs as well, and feel connected with the success of the business or enterprise. Engaged employees believe that what they do on the job is important and they feel they are valued for their work. This can make a huge difference in both their attitude and commitment to their jobs as well as in the quality of their work.

Key Factors for Engagement

Numerous critical factors need to exist for employee engagement to be successful. Understanding these factors can help you increase employee engagement in your organization or work group, enabling you as a leader to better meet the challenges you face on your job.

The working relationship that employees have with their bosses and supervisors makes a huge difference in the level of engagement that they feel as part of the organization. The most important factor for establishing greater employee engagement is building trust and respect between a supervisor or manager and those who report to him. This trust and respect begins with effective communication. A leader must be a good communicator, not only by sharing information important for employees to be able to perform their jobs, but also by being a good listener. A leader must respect the opinions of employees, especially concerning their expertise on their jobs. If someone spends as much time working on a job as each employee does, then it just makes sense that she will gain valuable and important insights into how that job could be best performed. Listening to employees' input and suggestions is an important part of becoming an engaged leader. A supervisor or manager also needs to "walk the talk," meaning he must do what he says he will do. A leader can't say one thing and do another if he expects to gain the respect of others—especially from employees.

Another key factor is thinking about the nature of the jobs that employees perform. **As a leader or supervisor, you need to think about how to make your employees' jobs more interesting, challenging, and ultimately rewarding.** Of course, there are inherent limitations in many jobs—some jobs won't appear to be challenging or interesting—but if you give this some creative thought, you can make a big difference. You should also consider asking employees how they feel their jobs could be made more challenging and productive. You might just be surprised how ingenious and innovative employees can be when given the opportunity to make suggestions about how their jobs could be more efficient and productive.

Employees also need to understand why their jobs are important and how they contribute to the company's overall performance. There is a reason why every job exists and a purpose for its existence. Surprisingly, employees often don't understand how their job fits into the bigger picture or why it is important on a higher level. When you provide the opportunity for employees to understand this, it can make a big difference in their level of commitment and dedication about how they perform their jobs. An employee can change how he perceives his job by visiting other parts of the organization or interacting more with the customers. Giving employees the chance to see how their work affects others, including the ultimate customer, helps them better understand the importance of their position.

Employees also need to have the ability to grow and develop in their jobs. Career growth is important to everyone. It doesn't necessarily mean a promotion—growth can exist even within an employee's current job. There are many skills, challenges, and opportunities that can become part of an existing job, although they are not listed as part of the current job description. You must encourage employees to think about how they can grow in their jobs, whether through a promotion or within their current position. This helps keep them motivated and working toward their future growth and development.

Employees feel they are important contributing members of the team when they are part of a group working together toward shared goals. They feel an identity and connection to the others and then work harder to help the team reach its goals. And, perhaps most importantly, they are able to accomplish more working together than as independent contributors in the organization.

Employees also should feel good about the organization where they work. People want to work for a company that has a good reputation in the community and the marketplace. Employees want to see their employer engaged in and working toward the greater good of the community and society. In this type of work culture, employees will want to contribute and enhance the company's good reputation. They want to identify with this reputation and feel that they are part of it as well.

As a leader, you play a very important role in helping make the changes needed to create a more engaged workplace. You then enjoy the many benefits that can be achieved as a result. The following 12 leadership actions are critically important to beginning this journey to a more engaged workplace. Each one of these actions sends an important message to employees that you are serious about changing the culture and their roles in the organization. The 12 actions help you create a collaborative workplace in which everyone benefits.

12 Leadership Actions for Greater Employee Engagement

1. **Lead by example.** You need to lead by example. You can't say you support one thing and act in a different way. If you expect employees to be open and honest with you about matters important to getting the work done, then you need to treat employees in the same way. Actions do speak louder than words, and actions will be the only thing that will convince employees you are true to your word and serious about employee engagement.

2. **Be willing to listen.** Employees have many thoughts and ideas about their jobs and how the work might be performed more efficiently. The extent that they share these ideas is directly related to the culture of the organization. If their experience in the past has been that nobody is particularly interested in their ideas or suggestions, they will stop offering them to their leaders. However, if their efforts to make insightful suggestions are listened to and acted upon, they will be much more likely to contribute their ideas. They will then feel as if they are being recognized. It is also important to listen to how employees feel about their role in the organization and what frustrates them. Everyone feels at some time that they may not be treated fairly at work. This is reality. But listening empathetically to employees and at least acknowledging these feelings can go a long way toward building stronger, more positive working relationships with those who report to you.

3. **Keep promises and commitments.** A leader needs to be careful not to make promises or commitments that she may not be able to keep. Leadership integrity is based upon being true to your word and living up to commitments. An engaged leader understands

this and makes sure not to make commitments she may not be able to keep later on. It would be much better to tell employees that you are not able to make a certain commitment than to make it and later have to go back on your word. Employees will at least emotionally hold you to your commitments and you will lose their trust if you don't deliver.

4. **Be supportive of your employees.** You need to be the strongest advocate for your employees, not their critic. Those who work for you need to believe that you are truly on their side and are willing to "go to bat for them" with others in the organization.

5. **Demonstrate a willingness to trust others.** If an employee is experienced and knowledgeable about his job, he requires less direct supervision and will appreciate the trust you place in him to do his job correctly without your direct involvement. This doesn't mean that he doesn't want to hear from you, because he does, but in a more collaborative manner instead of directive. This gives you more time to deal with other issues that do require your attention.

6. **Provide the resources necessary to do the job correctly.** It really isn't fair to expect employees to perform a job in which they haven't been given the resources necessary to complete it properly. As a supervisor or manager you need to ensure that employees do have these resources and that they receive the training to use these resources.

7. **Recognize good performance.** Simply saying "thanks" to someone in recognition for their good performance is important. It not only recognizes the employee, it also reinforces this behavior, making it more likely the behavior will be repeated in the future.

8. **Treat people with dignity.** It is important that a supervisor or manager treats those who report to her with dignity at all times, even if she is not being treated as such by an employee. You are held to a higher standard of behavior, especially when it comes to the way you treat those who work for you. Resorting to treating employees with anything less than dignity will cause you to ultimately lose their respect, regardless of your rationale. You will gain more respect by not resorting to such behavior and consistently treating others in a respectful manner.

9. **Get employees involved.** Facilitating employee participation, starting work teams, encouraging employees to get involved—all can jump-start your employee engagement initiatives. Employees do want to be more involved and will appreciate and enjoy being part of teams focused on improving their jobs and the workplace.

10. **Encourage creativity.** Allow and support employees to become more creative in their work. Encourage employees to become more innovative by providing suggestions about how things can be improved. Also, encourage employees to come up with ideas about things that may not have been done before. You never know what results you might achieve by becoming more innovative in your problem-solving process.

11. **Delegate responsibilities.** The reality is that you can't do everything yourself, no matter how hard and long you work on your job. The more you give away your responsibilities and even authority, the more you actually get back. Instead of just *your* efforts working on solving problems in the workplace, you can have many other people focused on these same things. This can help you become much more effective and productive as a leader.

12. **Be positive.** A leader sets the tone for the entire workplace. If a leader has a negative attitude about his job, the organization, top management, or anything else, this will likely be transferred to those who report to him. This negativity doesn't help these matters get any better and it probably makes things worse. As a leader, you need to set a positive tone that is supportive of the organization's efforts to achieve its goals and overall mission. You may not always agree with every decision or action that others make in the organization, but you should try to find ways to support the organization's initiatives. You only confuse employees by being critical about decisions and actions from the higher ups in the organization.

The Employee Engagement Difference

Employee engagement can mean many different things to different people. Employee engagement is about getting people more involved in their jobs. This involvement goes way beyond just getting employees to come to work each day. It is what happens after they come in the door that makes the difference between employees who are engaged at work or not. The difference between just showing up and being truly involved in your job can be extraordinary. Employee engagement begins with believing that each individual employee can make a difference and has something important to contribute to the whole. It is recognizing and respecting the expertise that each employee brings to his job. Unfortunately, in many work environments today, this is not the case, and many employees are not provided with opportunities to share their expertise and experience. This results in employees who are less motivated and less productive in their jobs. Think about the difference that having engaged employees can make. Imagine what it must be like to have employees who think about how they can perform their jobs better and more efficiently without you constantly trying to get them to do this. Picture just how much better you would be able to reach the goals and objectives of your job if you had more engaged employees reporting to you. This book will help you learn how you can actually achieve such a workplace. Each chapter reviews a different leadership benefit from creating such a workplace of employee engagement. As a result, you can become a more effective and successful leader.

GET MORE PLAYERS IN THE GAME

Imagine that you are the coach of a sports team and you suddenly have the ability to put more players in the game than the regulations allow. Just think of the competitive advantage you would have. Employee engagement can potentially give you this same competitive advantage as a leader. One of the most valuable benefits of employee engagement is that it helps get more employees involved in their jobs and fully using their skills, experience, and expertise. Employee engagement encourages employees to do more than just meet the minimal requirements of their job. Employees then have a greater sense of ownership over their jobs. In this sense, employee engagement gets more players in the game at work.

The really good news is that there are no regulations or officials dictating how many players you can have actively involved at work at any given time. The possibilities are endless. You can have all of your employees as active, engaged participants. Engaging your employees can get more people thinking about the problems and issues that you as a leader or supervisor must deal with at work on a regular basis. Many employees aren't fully engaged at work, most likely because they were never given the opportunity to be more involved. Engaging your employees changes this and provides these opportunities for them. More people can provide input into a problem or issue, so better decisions can be made. Employee engagement reminds us on a daily basis that "All of us are smarter than any one of us," including you, as the leader or supervisor of a group.

Employees *want* to be more active participants in their work by becoming fully engaged—they don't want to just go through the motions either. But they have to be given the opportunity to work in such an engaged environment, not simply put in their time. Surveys conducted by employers have consistently shown that many—if not most—employees in organizations are at the least "not engaged," and may even be disengaged when it comes to presently contributing as a team member. The question that should be asked in the survey is: Why are so many employees disengaged at work? The answer to this question may be found by looking at the leadership style of the supervisors. The level of employee engagement in an organization is directly related to the working relationships between supervisors and employees. Employee engagement begins with changing your employees' attitudes about their role in the organization, which can yield significantly positive, productive, and rewarding results.

Employees who work on a job regularly are going to have the most knowledge about how to make their job more efficient and productive, as well as having many other valuable insights. This is perhaps one of the greatest untapped resources in most organizations today. You should more fully utilize the talents and abilities of your employees from a productivity standpoint. Your employees will appreciate and feel good about you and their work as a result of your asking for their opinions. Everyone wants to feel like they are valuable and contributing members of any work group or team. This recognition is such an important part of getting employees more engaged in their work, as well as improving the problem-solving and decision-making processes in the workplace today. This gives employees a sense of job ownership that gets them more interested and committed to decisions that they participated in—they are no longer just spectators or perhaps even critics of the way the "game" is being played. Employee engagement gets employees off the bleachers and onto the field of play in your organization or workplace.

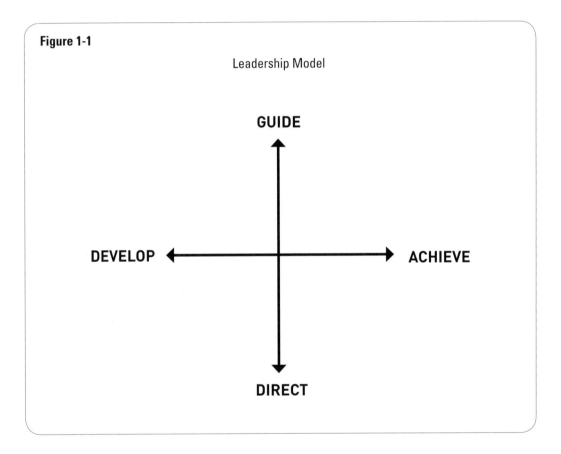

Figure 1-1

Leadership Model

GUIDE

DEVELOP ⟵⟶ **ACHIEVE**

DIRECT

In this model there are two continuums shown. Looking vertically at this model, you see the continuum of *guide* to *direct*. On the horizontal continuum, you see *develop* to *achieve*. These represent important leadership traits or characteristics that are present in one's leadership style. Some leaders have a greater propensity toward *developing* people and others are more focused on *achieving* results. Both can lead to reaching the same objective but in different ways. Similarly, some leaders are more prone to *guide* others toward reaching goals and others more comfortable being more *direct* in leading others to reach goals. Both can get you ultimately to the same place.

This model does not mean to imply that one of these leadership tendencies is better or worse, but rather identifies how these may influence a leader's ability to engage those employees who report to him. Each of these continuums represents important but differing leadership styles. Looking at the horizontal axis, you again see the leadership difference between developing the organization versus actually achieving results. The question is which is most important at that time. On one hand, if all you ever focus on is achievement, and you pay no attention to developing employees for future achievements, then what have you really accomplished? You may achieve your short-term goals, but at the expense of your long-term objectives.

Looking next at the vertical axis, you see the distinction between guiding and directing employees. Again, this may be a matter of a leader's propensity to encourage employees to proceed on a path of self-direction or discovery or to direct them to goals they are expected to achieve. This too may have long- and short-term benefits to both the leader and the organization.

Although one might think this model implies that *developing* and *guiding* employees are the most desirable leadership characteristics to create and maintain a culture of employee engagement in a workplace, this is not necessarily true. These tendencies would be most supportive of the concepts of employee engagement, but they are *not* the only way to create such a workplace culture. The fact is that leaders bring different styles to their jobs, which become their strengths, and likely allowed them to aspire to a supervisory position in the organization. Leaders must lead within their comfort zones and be consistent with their personality and leadership traits. To expect leaders to adapt a leadership style contradictory to their own personal style would be a mistake, and certainly not a successful strategy. Rather, leaders need to have a greater awareness of their personal leadership style, which can help them better understand how their style influences and supports the concepts of employee engagement. A leader with a directive style can become an engaged leader by understanding how to lead employee engagement by using this tendency to direct employees in this path. A leader with a results or goals focus can similarly help engage employees by teaching employees how to focus more on the goals they are to achieve. The following self-assessment will help you better understand your own leadership style and how it influences your ability to be an engaged leader.

Supervisor's Engagement Self-Assessment

It is important to take an introspective look at your own leadership style and see how it presently may or may not be supportive of creating a more engaged workplace. Some supervisors might not be aware that they are part of the problem because of their leadership style or behaviors. They may unintentionally inhibit or even discourage employees from engaging more in their jobs. This might be caused by many reasons, such as leadership styles, misunderstanding the concepts of employee engagement, and conflicting expectations of others including their bosses, organizational culture, and so on. You need to better understand how important your role is in employee engagement. This is critical to creating a workplace in which every employee wants to get more involved. The following *Supervisor Engagement Self-Assessment* can help you better understand your own employee engagement leadership style. Select the answer from the multiple choices presented that best describes how you would respond to or act as a leader in each of the following circumstances:

Supervisor Engagement Self-Assessment

1. An employee who reports to you is struggling to finish an important project that must be completed within a few days. Which of the following would best represent how you would deal with this situation?

    a. Provide guidance to the employee on how he could use his experience and knowledge to get his job done on time.

    b. Provide guidance to the employee on how to complete the project on time based on your experiences.

    c. Direct the employee on how he should complete the project.

    d. Due to the time constraint, specifically tell the employee exactly what needs to be done to complete the project on schedule.

2. Your work group needs to expand due to increased business demands that require a higher level of expertise and performance within your team. Which would be your most important priority?

    a. Explain to your existing employees the benefits of learning the new skills required as a result of this expansion to gain their interest.

    b. Encourage your existing employees to learn the skills necessary to perform these new responsibilities.

    c. Choose the best qualified existing employees in your work group to be trained on these new skills.

    d. Assign or hire the employees who have the skills and experience you need as a result of this expansion.

3. As a supervisor, you know the answer to a problem that your employee has been struggling to solve. Which of the following would you most likely do in this situation?

    a. Work with this person to help her discover the solution on her own, so that she learns how to deal better with these types of problems in the future.

    b. Provide guidance to the employee to help her find the solution.

    c. Direct the employee toward the correct solution without providing her with the answer to the problem.

    d. To save time in this situation, tell the employee the answer to the problem to ensure that it is solved immediately and explain to her why this was the best way to deal with the problem.

4. What do you think is the best way to supervise an experienced employee who has a high level of expertise on the job?

    a. Delegate the major decisions of the job based on her experience and expertise on the job.

    b. Provide guidance as needed by the employee to achieve desired results.

    c. Discuss with the employee areas she needs to develop in the future, providing guidance in this process.

    d. Listen to the input of the employee before making decisions related to that employee's job.

5. If you had to choose between the following resources, would you:

    a. Create training and development processes for employee development.

    b. Create specific on-the-job training to enable employees to perform their jobs better.

    c. Select certain employees for developmental assignments or training to help your work group perform at a higher level.

    d. Invest in process improvements to enhance product quality or customer service.

6. What do you think is the most important leadership characteristic today?

    a. Ensuring that each employee understands how to perform his job correctly.

    b. Helping every employee reach his greatest potential in the performance of his job.

    c. Developing a workforce able to meet the future challenges that the organization may face.

    d. Ensuring that everything you are responsible for is operating correctly and is supportive of the goals of the organization.

7. Who do you think should be held accountable for the results of a person's job?

    a. Primarily the employee, but also the supervisor.

    b. Primarily the supervisor, but also the employee.

    c. The employee.

    d. The supervisor.

8. Who do you believe should be given recognition for a work group achieving its goals?

    a. The employee.

    b. The entire work team.

    c. The supervisor and employees directly involved.

    d. The supervisor.

9. What do you believe is the most important goal to focus on in achieving a workplace based on employee engagement?

    a. Ensuring that every employee receives the training and information necessary to perform their jobs to the best of their ability.

    b. Adapting a culture that supports employees on all levels of the organization concerning becoming more involved and accountable for their jobs.

    c. Leadership that is supportive of the concepts of employee engagement.

    d. Measuring the results of employee engagement.

10. What do you think is the greatest benefit to a supervisor in moving toward achieving a workplace based on employee engagement?

    a. Employees reaching their highest potential, enabling them to perform their jobs better.

b. Greater employee job satisfaction, ultimately enabling the supervisor to lead more effectively.

c. Changing the culture of the organization to be more supportive of the concepts of employee engagement to help everyone—including supervisors—reach their shared goals for success.

d. The organization becoming better able to meet or exceed the requirements of their customers.

Self-Assessment Results

It is important to understand that there are no right or wrong answers to this self-assessment, but rather, its purpose is to help you better understand your leadership tendencies. You will be oriented toward the specific directions presented in the *Engaged Supervisor Model*. Looking at the selections you made on this self-assessment, you can find where your leadership style or characteristics would be on this model shown below with four quadrants identified based on the combinations of the leadership directions presented in the model. To gain a better understanding of your "engaged leadership" style, count the number of questions in the *Engagement Self-Assessment* that you answered as either a, b, c, or d and plot them in the *Engaged Leader Profiler* below to see where your leadership tendencies are in relation to each of these quadrants. For example, if the majority of your answers fall into quadrant A, this would indicate that you tend to be focused on guiding and developing those who report to you.

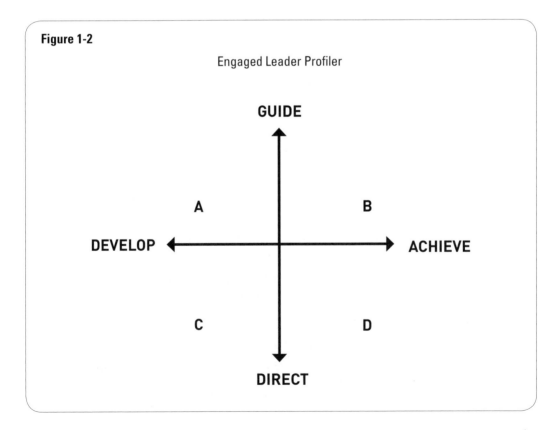

Figure 1-2

Engaged Leader Profiler

Case Study

Sometimes we have to be reminded just how important it is to keep everyone actively involved in their jobs to achieve the best results at work. In this brief story, the value of getting more employees involved in the "game" is realized by a new supervisor. She is reminded of the importance of asking your employees for their opinions and advice.

Alice Henderson had been the supervisor of the customer service group at the company's largest call center for the past two years. She actually began her career with the company as a customer service representative (CSR) more than 10 years ago, moving first to group leader, then section leader at the call center. Over the years, Alice had seen the call center grow from about 50 CSRs to more than 400, matching the growth in the industry. Alice enjoyed her leadership role that she had aspired to through her hard work over the years. She felt especially prepared for this level of supervisory responsibility as she had worked her way up through the ranks in the organization. As a result, she did have extensive first-hand experience and knowledge of the jobs of the CSRs who reported to her and the problems and challenges they faced on a daily basis, dealing with the calls they handle from prospective and existing customers of the company. However, paradoxically, sometimes this experience and knowledge seemed to be as much of a liability as it was a benefit to her as the leader of the group. Because of her confidence in her extensive knowledge of this function, she would make decisions without consulting anyone else, including the CSRs, as she believed she knew how they would feel about any issue. She felt she was accurately representing their interests.

The problem was that this assumption on her part was not always correct. It had been several years since Alice had actually sat in a CSR's chair and handled incoming calls. Even though she had been involved in making changes over time in the operating procedures of the call center, all of this experience had been from a supervisory perspective, not that of a CSR. This meant that Alice didn't always know what it was like to be currently working as a CSR at the call center, yet she was making many decisions daily based on her outdated experiences as a CSR. There was a growing frustration in the call center that the interests of the CSRs were no longer being understood by the leadership of the company, including Alice. This was becoming apparent to the top management of the company, especially as a result of a recent employee engagement survey in which CSRs were asked to comment on their feelings about their supervisor. The survey questioned the level of engagement CSRs felt they had in making decisions about matters which directly affected them and their ability to perform their jobs. The results of this survey indicated that Alice's direct reports felt they had very little input and that these types of decisions were being made almost exclusively at a level above them. Alice had thought she was doing a good job representing the CSRs interests, but was now realizing that she needed to change her leadership approach to such matters. This problem was not just that Alice received lower survey results than expected, but the performance index scores for her teams were also lower. This concerned Alice and her supervisor, who correctly associated both of these scores as related to one another.

Receiving these low survey scores was a somewhat shocking and emotional experience for Alice. As a CSR, she truly believed it was important for her voice to be heard about how to best serve their customers, and she realized she had forgotten this important principle. She also saw that the way she was currently trying to be a manager was creating a great deal of stress, not only for her, but apparently also for people in her group. They were increasingly frustrated with her leadership style. She remembered how infuriating it had been as a CSR to have great ideas about better serving the customer that were ignored. She had thought of solutions to work problems, but hadn't been listened to by her supervisor. Alice's intentions were good, but she wasn't giving her CSRs a chance to be engaged. She just assumed that based on her experience and expertise, she knew better than anyone what decisions to make or how to resolve problems on her team. Even though she did have a great deal of firsthand experience in such matters, she was not one of the people currently working closest to the problems, and therefore was not in the best position to make many of the decisions. Alice realized she was taking on the burden of making all the important decisions at work without asking those who were in a better position to provide her guidance. She wasn't truly using the most valuable resources that the company had provided her to help her perform her job. Instead, she was working literally day and night to try to solve all of these problems on her own without achieving the best results. Alice realized that she could not only make her job easier and much less frustrating, but she could also improve the jobs of her employees, by getting them more engaged in the decision-making and problem-solving process in their workplace.

From this story, think about how Alice was trying to do everything herself rather than engaging others, which actually caused her to be less effective on her job. Sometimes when you believe you are the only one who can or should make decisions, it actually makes you far less productive. Alice assumed that because she had previously performed the same job as her employees, she was the best person to make decisions about workplace issues. But what Alice quickly learned is that although she had prior experience on this job, those who were currently performing the job were still in a better position than she was to provide the best input into decisions about their jobs. This can be a difficult transition for any supervisor, especially in the situation which Alice found herself.

 WIIFM?

A fair question for you to ask as you explore the concepts and principles of employee engagement being introduced into your organization is: "What's in it for me (WIIFM)?"

Are the advantages of employee engagement focused solely on employees who are becoming more engaged, and not on you as their supervisor? To answer this question, think about some of the advantages for you if you are able to get "more players in the game," as this chapter discusses.

Think about the following questions.

1. Will employee engagement make your job more rewarding and even easier?

   _____

2. What impact could it have on your job if your employees were able to perform their jobs at a higher level of performance than they are presently?

   _____

3. What would be the benefits to you? List some of these that come to mind below.

   _____

   _____

   _____

ENGAGEMENT TIPS

- Make sure that everyone understands what you are trying to accomplish by introducing the concepts of employee engagement in the workplace.

- Make sure everyone understands their new roles and what will be expected of them in such a working environment.

- Allow employees to express their concerns about these changes.

- Describe these changes in terms of the advantages to each employee so they understand what's in it for them.

- Help everyone in your organization understand the advantage of multiple perspectives.

- There is a great value in asking employees on all levels of the organization: "What do you think?" Try it!

Leadership Challenge

1. What advantages could you gain if those who report to you are able to accept greater levels of responsibility and decisions? Think about the opportunities for you to focus on other responsibilities that could help you perform your job at a higher level. List some of these below:

   _____

   _____

   _____

2. How different do you believe your employees' attitudes about their jobs would be if they were to become more engaged in their jobs?

_____

_____

_____

• •

💡 Leader Action Planner

1. Think about opportunities to get those who report to you more involved in their jobs and in helping achieve the goals of the organization. What would some of those be?

_____

_____

_____

2. What are some of the things that you would need to consider to allow employees to become more engaged in their jobs?

_____

_____

_____

MAKE WORK
MORE INTERESTING

One of the greatest benefits of employee engagement is that it makes work more interesting for everyone. Employee engagement can challenge employees in ways they never experienced in the past. This concept can be applied to virtually any job or workplace. Regardless of the complexity of a job, there will always be aspects of that job that are normally someone else's responsibility. Moving these challenges into an employee's area of responsibility can create new or renewed interest in his job. This can make a supervisor or manager's job easier because she doesn't have to be the only one trying to motivate the employees—they are self-motivated by the challenges that being engaged can present to them.

But what really makes someone's job interesting? To answer this question, let's first think about some things people do away from the workplace that they enjoy, such as their hobbies or favorite pastimes. What makes these activities interesting or fun? For example, think about sports that people participate in on a regular basis—specifically, the game of golf. Golfers are often very passionate about this activity and seek it out every chance they get. When you think about it, this game really involves someone trying to propel a tiny round object in a straight path forward toward a specific destination, using the force of a special device they must swing in a very specific manner, repeating this process hopefully as few times as possible in specially designated areas. They must normally repeat this process 18 times as they walk across often difficult terrain, which contains obstacles, traps, and hazards such as water, sand, and trees to make it even harder. If the golfer does not comply with all the rules of this activity, she is penalized. The equipment that a golfer must use to complete these tasks is usually expensive, heavy, and bulky, which must be carried around for many miles or transported by an electric cart that the golfer normally must rent from the establishment where this activity is held. Engaging in this activity is often a very frustrating experience, as it requires a special skill and expensive training to improve performance, and it is not unusual for participants to get extremely angry, sometimes throwing these expensive pieces of equipment around, and even using profanity when their performance does not meet their expectations. Perhaps the most curious thing about this activity is that people are not paid to perform these tasks but rather pay to participate in it!

Of course, golfers play the game because they actually enjoy it. But what makes a golfer enjoy being engaged in something that can sound more like something to avoid rather than seek out? Let's examine some of these elements of the game that make it fun to play for golfers:

- **Challenge.** Golfers are constantly challenging themselves to try to improve their performance. They set goals for themselves on how they hope to improve by constantly increasing their performance level. They study this subject by reading golfing books and magazines, watching others who are professionals in the sport, and taking lessons.

- **Motivation.** Perhaps as a result of the challenging nature of the sport, golfers are typically very self-motivated to improve every time they play. They are typically willing or even eager to play this game in their quest to better their scores, and they get great satisfaction from even the slightest positive improvements in their performance.

- **Maintenance.** Golf is inherently a difficult sport to learn and particularly to become proficient at playing. Just learning to play this game at a higher level of performance doesn't guarantee that a golfer can maintain this level of performance. This makes playing well even more satisfying when it is achieved.

- **Support.** Golfers provide each other support and encouragement as they play the game together. They often compliment each other's shots (sometimes when it is really deserved). They even give advice to one another (usually unsolicited) to try to help each other improve their performances.

- **Scoring.** Golfers keep precise (sometimes) score of how they play each round to measure their performance against previous performances. They keep track of these scores, often sharing them with other golfers and noting when they have performed particularly well. Sometimes scores are collected over time and calculated in terms of performance against a standard of performance called a *handicap*, which provides another level of comparison between different golfers' varying skills.

- **Recognition.** Golfers often recognize others' good performances by commenting on particularly high levels of performance. Sometimes this recognition is formal and public, such as the presentation of awards or trophies for winning.

- **Camaraderie.** Golf is typically played in foursomes together. These groups often play together regularly, sometimes for years. As each player takes his turns hitting his ball, the others provide encouragement and support. Golfers not only enjoy playing the sport but also enjoy being involved in an activity with others who have the same interest in playing the sport as they do.

Now, think about how these same things that make a favorite pastime such as playing golf could make your workplace more enjoyable and engaging; think about how your own job could become more satisfying if these things were part of your workplace.

- **Challenge.** Think about how challenging your employees' jobs are for each of them. Are they currently challenged by their work? Challenge makes activities more interesting. Challenge gives an employee something to strive for to achieve in the future. People need to be challenged to stay interested in their jobs. Challenge doesn't necessarily mean just giving someone more work—which may not be challenging but rather frustrating to the employee—instead, it means providing more challenging goals and objectives for employees to obtain. It is highly satisfying for someone to stretch to achieve a goal previously thought unobtainable. Engaging employees involves giving those who report to you more challenging but achievable assignments that they'll feel a sense of accomplishment completing. However, if you provide challenges to employees who are not ready to accept them, they can become highly frustrated, particularly if they feel they have not been provided the necessary resources to meet these challenges. These resources may include training, access to information, and so on—whatever is needed to meet these challenges.

Think about how you could be more challenged in your job. How can creating a more engaged workplace create a more satisfying work experience and result for you?

- **Motivation.** As in golf, motivation must come from within an individual. You can't force someone to become motivated. However, as a supervisor or manager, you can *help* employees to become motivated by creating reasons why they should become motivated to perform their jobs better. Providing challenges (as mentioned above) is one way to motivate employees. Providing incentives such as recognition or rewards can also provide motivation to employees. Perhaps the best way to motivate employees is to find out what really interests them about their jobs and to provide these opportunities to them when possible.

- **Support.** Being supportive of those who work for you is critically important in the engagement process. Employees need to feel that their supervisor—as well as the organization—supports them in their work and careers. They need to feel that someone has their best interests in mind, that someone has their back. Support comes in many different ways and forms. It can simply be the encouragement of a supervisor as employees are given the opportunity to make a greater contribution in their jobs. Support could also be providing the resources that engaged employees need to meet these challenges. Employees will not feel engaged if they don't sense that they have this support, and may even become disengaged if they feel otherwise. Employees may see the amount of support they receive as the true measure of the organization's commitment to the concept of employee engagement.

- **Scoring.** Every sport involves some kind of scoring or measurement of performance. It might be the amount of points that each team has earned, the time it takes to complete an athletic activity, the distance that an object can be propelled, or many other measures. As illustrated in the previous golf example, one of the things that makes golf interesting and enjoyable is keeping score to measure one's performance currently and over time to track improvements. Just think how different any sport would be if there wasn't some kind of score or time measurement. Would a golfer still feel challenged and interested in the game if she didn't keep score? Work can be made more interesting and engaging if there are accurate measures of performance and employees are encouraged to improve their performance against these measures.

- **Recognition.** Recognizing improved or improving performance is essential to creating a more engaged workplace and workforce. Everyone needs recognition and to be rewarded for their accomplishments. Recognition and rewards are what motivates employees to become more engaged. Employees become disengaged when they feel they aren't being recognized or rewarded for their hard work and accomplishments, and this is especially true when it comes to their supervisor. Recognition can come in many different forms. It can be formal, such as award programs sponsored by the organization that single out exceptional performance of individuals and groups. It can also be informal, such as a simple "thank you" or acknowledgment of employees' extra efforts.

Think about how much recognition there is in your workplace or work group. Do you think that those who work for you feel they are receiving the recognition and rewards they deserve? How do you think those who work for you would respond to receiving more recognition than they presently receive? How do you think this would affect your role as their leader if your work group felt more recognized?

- **Camaraderie.** People enjoy being part of a team in which everyone is working together toward shared goals. They enjoy the relationships that are developed in the process. Just think about the many potential benefits of increasing teamwork in your work group or organization. Teamwork creates greater synergies in an organization because employees who work well together can achieve much more than employees working independently. Chapter 4 will review the many benefits of creating greater teamwork in an organization in more detail.

Getting Employees Excited About Work Again

It is common for employees to lose the interest they once had in their jobs because it no longer provides many of the things mentioned above. At one time they may have been excited about their work and felt a sense of accomplishment and satisfaction, but as time passed, their job became something they had to do to earn a paycheck. Supervising employees with this attitude can be difficult and frustrating. It may seem like you are constantly trying to get employees to do what you expect them to be doing on their own. Imagine how much easier and less frustrating it would be to lead others who were more interested, even excited, about their jobs again. Think about how much more effectively they could perform their jobs and consequently how much better you could perform your job if those who reported to you were interested in their jobs. Think about how much you could accomplish. You might even get more excited about your own job than you have been for a long time!

So what can you do to get employees excited about their jobs again? The following are five keys to getting employees interested and even excited about their jobs again.

Expanding Employees' Interest in Their Jobs

Looking at Figure 2-1, you can see the overall job responsibilities shown in relation to the parts of the job that really interest this employee. This is actually a model for employee disengagement. In this example, this employee's interests are outside the overall responsibilities of the job. This is not an unusual situation in which many employees find themselves. For various reasons, employees feel stuck in a job that is of little or no real interest to them or is not consistent with the type of job responsibilities they would actually enjoy performing. In many situations, there is not much that can be done to address this problem, but it is still the cause of many disengaged employees who are uninterested in their work in general. If this is a problem in your workplace, the more you are able to address

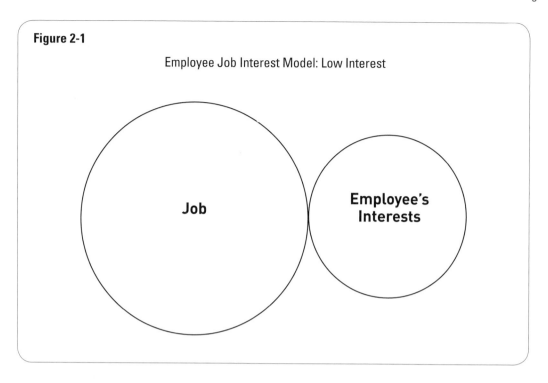

Figure 2-1

Employee Job Interest Model: Low Interest

Job

Employee's Interests

and move toward correcting this situation, the more engaged your employees will become in their jobs. But don't despair—there are many things you can do to address this problem.

In this view, the employee's interests are obviously outside the responsibilities and scope of the job. There may not be much that can be done to change this situation (based on the nature of the job) for it to be compatible with the particular interests of the incumbent in the job. However, thinking creatively, you may be able to find ways to channel these personal interests into the employee's job, as his supervisor. If you can do this, you will find that this individual will be much more engaged and excited about the job.

In this model shown in Figure 2-2, the employee's interests are still mostly outside the scope of the job responsibilities, but there is now more overlap with the job. This model begins to move toward employee engagement. When employees are more interested in their jobs, they will become more engaged both in the short- and long-term. The more the job and an employee's interests are connected, the more connected the employee will feel about their job. Finding ways to both identify and utilize your employees' interests in their job is one of the secrets to creating a more engaged workforce.

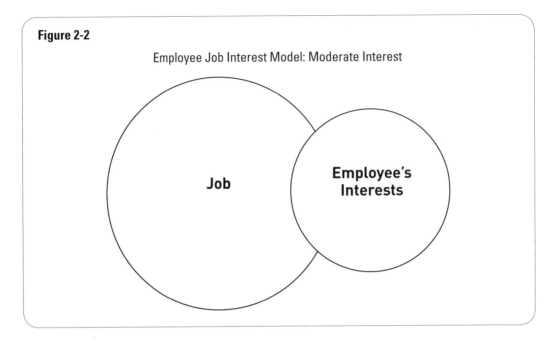

Figure 2-2

Employee Job Interest Model: Moderate Interest

Job

Employee's Interests

Finally, Figure 2-3 shows a situation in which an employee's interests are being fully incorporated into the job. In this model, the employee is doing what he is most interested in during the course of performing the job. This naturally leads to employees who are more engaged and excited about their jobs. This is the scenario when you often hear employees express how much they enjoy their jobs and how they feel fulfilled by performing these duties and responsibilities. Again, you may not always be able to reach this level of job interest with your employees, but the closer you can come, the more engaged they will be as a result.

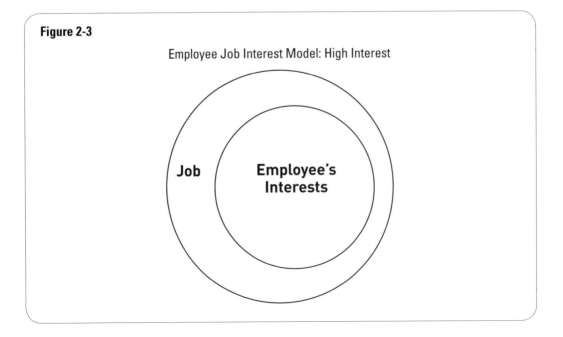

Figure 2-3

Employee Job Interest Model: High Interest

Job

Employee's Interests

One of the ways to address this issue is to think about job fit. Do you have the employee in the right job that best matches her skills and interests? If the answer is no, then you should first be thinking about how this problem could be addressed. Is there some other job that this person could be placed in that would be a better fit given this situation? If not, is there a way to change certain aspects of this job which would allow this employee to become more interested in the job? Are there certain responsibilities that could be expanded or redirected toward this person that would use his talents and interests better? Could some of the responsibilities of this job be redirected to another employee, which might be more aligned with her interests and talents?

Employees Enjoy Doing What Is of Most Interest to Them

Think about the following things when considering how to bring out your employees' talents and interests concerning their jobs:

- Think about the strengths and interests, talents, experiences, training, expertise, and so on that each person who works for you brings to their job.

- Think about how much more interested in their job your employees would be if given the opportunity to do these things that they are most interested in concerning their job.

- Have you ever talked to each of your employees about what it is that they would really like to do more or learn to do in their job?

- Think about how you can help develop the strengths of your employees to allow them to make a greater contribution to their job.

- Think about how you could better use these attributes of each of your employees that they bring to their job.

- Think about the benefits of developing these strengths of your employees to both your employees and the organization.

- Think about how employees could share their expertise and abilities with others.

- Think about how better using the talents of your employees could open up other career possibilities for them.

- Think about how much more innovative employees might be if they were interested in their job.

- Think about how less likely employees might be to leave the organization if they were encouraged to build on their strengths in performing their job.

Too often, we focus on what individuals need to improve on rather than what they excel in and do well. This may have the effect of moving the amount of interest an employee has in his job further outside the scope of the job. The employee begins to think more about what he would really like to be doing in his career and less about the actual job he has to perform. Again, think about how much more productive people would be if you put less energy into correcting their weaknesses, and instead put this effort into developing their strengths. If you focus on someone's weaknesses, you will only bring this level of performance to an average or an acceptable level at best. But if you focus on developing someone's strengths, you can realistically expect to get excellent job performance as a result, because you are now playing to that person's strengths. It just makes sense that employees will be more interested in work they enjoy doing and are good at performing. It feels good to do something well and when you get praise and recognition too, it is all the better.

Think of yourself as a coach of a sports team. You would assess the talents, skills, and interests of each of your players in assigning them to certain positions. For instance, it just wouldn't make any sense to assign someone who has an interest in passing the football into a lineman's position or a defensive position. Doing so would not only frustrate the aspiring quarterback, but also the other players who might be required to play quarterback who also may be disinterested in that role. The same is true in assigning your employees to roles and positions on your work team when you have the discretion to do so. Finding the right role for employees can be an important part of creating an engaged workplace for everyone.

Sometimes it might not be possible to assign someone a job which best fits their interests for many valid reasons. In these circumstances, are there *elements* of the job which you could encourage or assign an employee to perform which *are* consistent with their talents and interests? For example, you could have an employee who is very good at artwork but the nature of the work has nothing to do with anything artistic or creative. You should consider if there are opportunities at work outside—of his job itself—in which this employee's artistic abilities could be used, for instance the company newsletter, company brochures, even murals in the workplace. The more creative you can be, the better. Think about how this employee might appreciate being asked to draw something in one of these venues and the recognition she might receive from co-workers as a result, not to mention her self-satisfaction. What about a person who has an interest in writing or photography? Could you channel these interests in similar ways, such as the company newsletter or brochures, and so on? Could employees' interest in sports be channeled in company golf or softball teams or tournaments? Even better is when you can find ways to channel these interests somehow in their jobs, such as developing programs or contests with sports themes. Think about how you can channel as many of your employees' personal interests that could be used at work. These are the type of activities that get people engaged. Think about the benefits to you by getting those who work for you more interested in their work. How much more of a contribution do you think they will make to the goals of your organization? How much different of a work environment do you think this type of engagement would create? Think about how getting employees interested and even excited about their jobs and work could make supervising them easier and more productive.

Case Study

Jonathan Simpson was the supervisor of a group of 10 accountants working for a small financial services company. Jonathan sensed that people in his group were not fully engaged in their jobs. Yes, they performed their jobs the way they were expected to, even exceeding his expectations most of the time. Yet he had the sense that there was something missing in the overall job satisfaction of his group. Perhaps, he thought, it was the work itself, which could be very routine and detail-oriented. But that was the nature of their jobs and he believed that everyone in his group enjoyed working in accounting because they often expressed this to him. Still, he wondered why everyone seemed so disengaged in other ways at their jobs.

Jonathan expressed his concerns to his human resource manager, who suggested that he consider introducing the concepts of employee engagement into his work group. The human resource manager offered Jonathan a book about leading employee engagement and he quickly became interested in the subject. One of the things the book suggested was to ask employees for their suggestions about how the workplace could be made more engaging to them. It suggested that allowing employees to use their skills and interests as they could relate to their jobs or just the workplace would help get them more engaged. Jonathan immediately decided to give this approach a try. The next morning he called a meeting for all of his employees to introduce this idea and ask them for their suggestions on how to proceed. He was quite surprised at their response.

Jonathan began by explaining that he had recently learned about employee engagement. He learned that providing opportunities for employees to do what they were most inter-ested in could change how they felt about their work. He was about to qualify this state-ment by acknowledging that the nature of their accounting work may not particularly lend itself to this type of concept when several members of the work group began to speak up.

"I think that's a great idea!" Mary Simpson responded. Mary was normally a very quiet person who always did a good job but never really did more than she was asked to do, so Jonathan was quite surprised by her reaction. "I've been thinking recently that there are many things we could do that would not only make our jobs more interesting but more efficient as well," Mary added.

"What are your suggestions?" asked Jonathan, anxious to hear what she was thinking.

"Well, for one thing I think that our work area looks drab!" Mary replied, getting a laugh from everyone.

"OK, what would you suggest we do to improve our drabness?" said Jonathan.

"I have always been interested in interior design and decorating and would love to have the opportunity to make this a warmer and more comfortable work environment for all of us. I would really like to get rid of all the 'institutional grey' that's around here every-where. I would be happy to give you some rough sketches to consider. It really wouldn't cost very much to make a big difference in the appearance of our work areas," Mary responded enthusiastically.

"Yeah, that would be great, but I think it would be a better idea if we formed a team to re-view your ideas to get more people's input." Jonathan suggested, clearly beginning to get the idea of what employee engagement is all about.

"Who would like to participate in this team?" he asked. Nearly everyone in the group raised their hands. He hadn't ever seen this much enthusiasm among his employees on anything they had worked on previously. Jonathan knew that he was on to something that was going to have a very positive impact on his work group and ultimately his leadership.

· ·

 **WIIFM?**

1. What do you think would be the potential benefits to you of having your employees become more interested in their jobs than they may be presently?

    _____

    _____

    _____

ENGAGEMENT TIPS

- Ask for employees' input on how you can get them involved in aspects of their jobs or contributing in other ways which would allow them to use their personal interests.

- See if there are other parts of your organization that have had success in these types of activities. It might be easier for you to "sell" this idea if it has already been successful in another part of your organization.

- Read about how other organizations may have tapped into their employees' personal interests through books, magazines, Internet searches, and so on.

- Tapping into employees' interests should not be restricted to just their jobs. Employees will be interested in other ways to bring their personal interests into work. Here are just a few suggestions:

    - **Personal Computing.** Establish computer clubs in which your employees who are particularly interested in personal computers can share their interests together. They might just come up with suggestions that could be useful at work.

    - **Community Service.** Support a local charitable or nonprofit organization that employees are interested in serving. Provide work time opportunities to serve these organizations or facilities to help them in their work.

    - **Athletic Events.** Establish golf or bowling teams, softball tournaments, bike rides, 5K fun runs or walks, and so on.

    - **Car Clubs.** Encourage employees to bring in their collectible cars to work.

    - **Family Days.** Sponsor a family day celebration in which employees are permitted to bring their families to the facility to see where their loved ones work.

Leadership Challenge

Think about how giving those who report to you the opportunity to use their personal interests and skills on their jobs could help make the workplace more efficient and an even more enjoyable place to work.

1. What do you think would be some of these benefits?

    _____

    _____

    _____

Leader Action Planner

1. How can you better tap into your employees' personal interests to get them more engaged at work? List ideas below:

    _____

    _____

    _____

2. How can you get started?

    _____

    _____

    _____

CHAPTER 3

HELP EMPLOYEES UNDERSTAND HOW THEIR JOB FITS INTO THE BIG PICTURE

Employee Engagement Mission Statement

Our mission is to create a more engaged workplace for all employees of the organization. To achieve this goal, we must establish positive work relationships between all levels of employees, sustaining clear, honest, and reliable communication for everyone. We will strive to provide every employee the opportunity to be successful in his career and provide fair and meaningful rewards and recognition for everyone. Employees will be allowed greater control of their personal development and careers and we will encourage everyone to provide input into how their jobs are to be performed. The values and principles of the organization will be frequently reviewed with employees on all levels of the organization. All employees will be given the opportunity to provide input on how they believe these values and principles are being followed and if they align with the daily management and operation of the organization. Our goal is for all employees to feel a shared sense of ownership and commitment to the performance of the organization, including a focus on meeting and exceeding the needs and expectations of customers.

Think about how this *Employee Engagement Mission Statement* could help create the organizational culture that would enable greater employee engagement to exist in your organization. What this mission encourages is for employees to think beyond their current job responsibilities to what occurs in the entire organization; or in other words, to think outside their job. As stated in this mission, it is important that everyone who works for you has a sense of ownership for the performance of the entire organization and a focus on the ultimate customer.

Think about the perspective that you have of the organization as a supervisor or manager. In your job you need to look at a broader perspective. You see how each employee's job fits into the bigger picture and how each person's job is important to the other jobs in the organization. You think about how employees can work better together to enable each other to perform their jobs and how the organization as a whole can operate more effectively to achieve its goals and objectives.

Now think about your employee's perspective of his job and the organization as a whole. What does he focus on as he performs his job? Most likely, he is focused mostly or entirely on his own job. He may not be thinking about the broader perspective that you have in your role as a supervisor or manager. His concern is probably primarily on his own work and not so much on how his work affects other employees' jobs or ultimately, the customer.

Your employees can easily lose sight as to how their job fits into or is important to the final product or service of the organization. Regardless of their role in the organization, their work can still seem insignificant or unimportant if they don't have the opportunity to see this bigger picture. Employees on all levels need to understand just how critically important their work is to the organization as a whole. Introducing employee engagement can help employees gain a better understanding of this broader view of where their jobs fit into the process. They will begin to see their jobs in much the same way as their supervisor or manager, looking at how they fit into the entire process rather than just a single function. This makes the supervisor or manager's job easier as their employees begin to view the workplace more holistically, understanding just how important their jobs really are to the end product or service of the organization.

For example, consider a carpenter, working on a project, who had a foreman who never told him what the end product was supposed to look like. The foreman did not show him the plans or any drawings of what the finished project would look like in the end. The carpenter satisfied the requirements of his job, given the limited information he received about his work. When the project was completed, however, and he saw the end result, he realized that if he had been told about the end goal, he could have performed his job differently to help better achieve this final objective—without having to work any harder or use any additional resources.

Think about how much information you share with your employees about the end product of the work they perform, and ask yourself if it is enough. What if your employees had the same access to information that you do to make decisions about their work and the workplace? Do you think they would make the same decisions as you? What would happen if you began to share this level of information as appropriate? What difference do you think this would make? Think about how providing your employees with more information as it relates to their jobs could enable them to do a better job. What would be the benefits to you of expanding the scope and understanding that employees have about the operation and functions of your organization?

In Figure 3-1, we see how an employee typically understands her job in relation to the rest of the organization. In this limited perspective, the employee basically only has a good vision of her job (shown as A) and perhaps those jobs with which she has the most direct contact (B). Think about the levels C, D, and E, as shown in this model. What perspective does this employee have of these jobs? How important is it that employees have this broader perspective about their jobs and understand how they fit into the bigger picture in the organization?

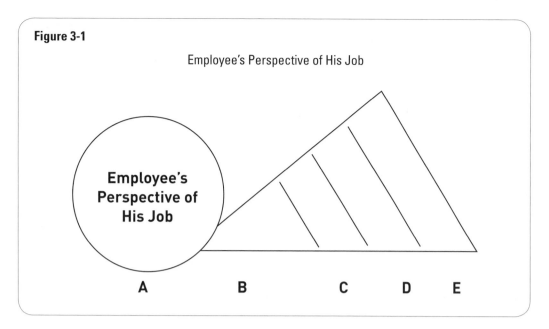

Figure 3-1

Employee's Perspective of His Job

Employee's Perspective of His Job

A   B   C   D   E

The following is an example of how the lack of this broader perspective can be a limiting factor for an employee as he performs the responsibilities of his job.

• •

 **Case Study**

The employees at Ace Manufacturing each had very specific job assignments as production workers. A product would move from one work station to the next as each employee added certain components to the product as part of the assembly process. The production area was designed with walls between each station, which were intended to reduce noise and other interferences between jobs. Although this design did accomplish this objective, it also prevented almost any communication between employees during the process. Compounding this problem, each department in the manufacturing process was located in a different part of the facility, with its own physical barriers separating it from the other production areas of the plant. This created separateness between employees in each production area, and even more between each production department. The result was that employees had no knowledge of what was occurring in other parts of the plant during the manufacturing process, and no vision of how their work affected others as the product moved to other areas toward its final assembly. What Ace Manufacturing thought was creating an efficient work process was in actuality creating barriers that greatly inhibited not only communication between employees and even departments, but also inhibited awareness of how each employee's job was important to the final product.

The plant manager was becoming concerned about some serious quality problems reported by customers, as returns from the field were beginning to significantly increase. He noticed this was a trend that had been occurring for many years, but had not been adequately addressed. There had been several initiatives to try to trace back to where the quality problems originated in the process, and corrective actions were put in place, but nothing was done to truly identify the root cause of this problem. For some reason, no one had identified the separate nature of the locations and work as the cause of these problems. It only happened when a production worker stopped the plant manager as he was walking through the factory one afternoon and suggested to him that the quality problem was being created by this design of the manufacturing process. It was as if a lightning bolt hit the manager. It just made so much sense once this problem's real root cause was identified to him.

He immediately realized how the design of the plant was preventing employees from understanding how each of their individual jobs fit into the final product. Each employee was basically isolated from the rest of the process and employees. Employees had little or no understanding of how the way they performed their jobs affected the next work station the product moved to in the production process. As he began to discuss this problem with more employees, he realized that many of the quality problems could be fairly easily prevented if employees had a better understanding of how the way they performed their jobs affected the subsequent steps in the process. He was amazed at how much time and effort was being expended reworking the product as a result of this lack of communication and visibility between job stations. Employees were basically working in the dark when it came to making certain decisions about how they performed their responsibilities at their step in the process. A subtle difference, such as the positioning of the product as it is moved ahead to the next work station in the process, could make a big difference in the efficiency of the operation. Positioning the product in alignment with the way the next employee needs it to be placed saves delays in the process and makes that employee's job easier to perform. As the plant manager was beginning to understand, employees didn't understand the connection between their job and the operation of the rest of the organization. In most cases, each employee could just as easily perform their job in such a way that would make the next employee's job easier to complete, if they only understood what to do to allow this to happen.

The plant manager's first instinct was to call his department heads together and tell them to develop a plan to correct this problem. However, as he thought about how this discovery had come to him, he began to realize this might not be the best way to solve this problem. After all, who would know better than those performing these jobs what needed to be done to make the process more efficient? He realized that he needed to get his management team involved, and the employees themselves. So he set up a team consisting of both groups that would develop a plan to redesign the production process to allow each employee to better understand how his job was important to producing a quality final product. At Ace Manufacturing, without realizing it, this was also the beginning of their employee engagement process.

Upstream/Downstream Job Integration

What was needed at Ace Manufacturing was actually upstream and downstream job integration. Employees need to have an appreciation for what happens both before and after they perform their job as it concerns the product—or in other cases, the services being provided to the customer. Depicted below is a view of this upstream/downstream job integration.

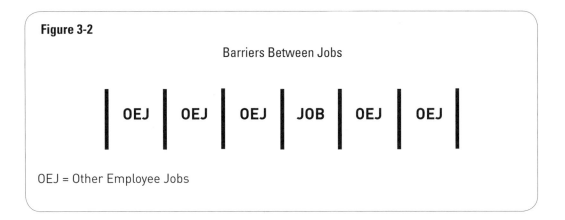

Figure 3-2

Barriers Between Jobs

OEJ = Other Employee Jobs

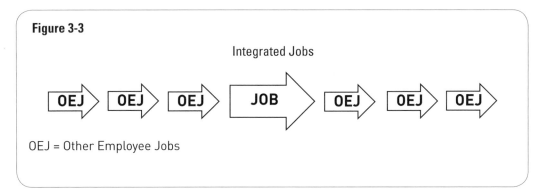

Figure 3-3

Integrated Jobs

OEJ = Other Employee Jobs

In a manufacturing process such as the case at Ace Manufacturing, envisioning this integration as fairly simple illustrations is a bit easier. In this case, there are distinct and sequential steps in the manufacturing process. At Ace Manufacturing, employees were working in isolation due to numerous factors, including the physical design of the manufacturing process. In this example, it was shown just how important it is for employees to have this understanding or vision of each other's jobs both before and after they perform their jobs. In this situation, product handoffs should be like a relay race, with runners passing the baton to one another to enable smooth and seamless transitions between jobs. Even in non-manufacturing types of jobs, the handoffs between job processes should be handled smoothly and effectively, establishing necessary context.

Understanding what happens in the work process both before and after a person performs her job enables that employee to do a better job, more completely. When she gains an appreciation for how others' job performances influence her ultimate job performance, it makes all the difference. Simply becoming more aware of these factors can be enlightening, as in the story about employees at Ace Manufacturing. Realizing how you may be affecting someone else's job in your work can save the next person a great deal of work and frustration, not to mention how it improves the ultimate quality of the product or service being provided.

Moving Away From Job Tunnel Vision

Here is a different story of an employee who worked at a manufacturing facility for nearly 39 years, where batch material was heated and then immediately transferred to the cold end of the process where it was formed into a final product. He spent his entire career in the hot end of the process. These two different operations each had distinct functions, but were connected because the product needed to be transferred quickly to the cold end of the process while still hot, so that it could be molded. Curiously, this particular employee hadn't ever visited or seen the cold end of the process. Each day of his career he came in an employee entrance at the hot end of the facility and never was given the opportunity or the occasion to step foot in the cold end of the factory. The plant manager heard about this situation on this employee's last day before retiring and personally escorted him to the cold end of the process to show him this part of the operation. The employee was amazed at what he saw during this visit to the "other side." He realized there were many things he could have done over his nearly four decades of sending hot materials to this cold end, which could have made others' jobs more efficient and easier if he had only known. All agreed that it was almost a tragedy he never saw this part of the operation until the last day of his long career.

Think about how this concept of upstream/downstream job integration can help you in your role as a supervisor or manager. What value could be added to your work processes by creating a work environment in which employees gain a better appreciation for each others' roles and responsibilities? How could this help improve the performance of each employee? What would be the value of this increased employee vision that could add to the ultimate success of your operation or function?

For example, think about how processes in your operation could be made more efficient and less redundant. What paperwork is currently required that may not really be needed or could be routed to fewer employees? What approvals may be currently required that do not need to be required? What similar tasks are being performed by different employees that could be consolidated? What problems are currently allowed, without finding the root cause and correcting it, so that employees don't have to deal with them over and over?

Perhaps even more importantly, what suggestions or recommendations might your employees have to improve not only their jobs but also how their jobs interact with other employee jobs to make your operation more efficient?

There are countless other examples of when employees gain this better understanding of how their jobs affect the jobs of others. Factors or functions such as labeling, speed, delivery, accuracy, consistency, communication, maintenance, and many other factors all can be significantly improved when employees gain this better understanding of how their jobs interrelate.

Collaboration Job Model

It is customary for most organizations to create specific jobs, each with its own purpose and function. Jobs are typically designed as independent entities specific to a particular function or area of the organization with certain qualifications required for incumbency in these roles. Distinguishing or separating these jobs further forms the hierarchical relationship that jobs have to one another in the organization. Jobs are evaluated in relationship to one another by such factors as the skills required to perform the job, responsibility assigned to the role, accountability of the position, and many others. Inherent in this design is a job independence that distinguishes each job incumbent's performance in relation to each other's. As a result, everyone sees each particular specific job independently of one another.

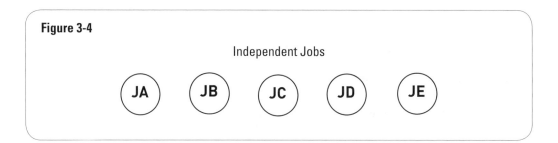

Figure 3-4

Independent Jobs

In Figure 3-4 (identified as Job A or JA, Job B or JB, and so on), we see the typical relationship between jobs that exists in most organizations. Each incumbent in each position works essentially independent of one another in this typical organizational design, except for occasional collaboration, as these jobs may at times share common objectives on certain projects, or may hand off work in the process.

But what if you were to look at your organization or function differently? What if you moved away from this traditional job design to one that would inherently create better communication and encourage more interaction between incumbents in these positions? In Figure 3-4, you can see a view of a different job design in which jobs are engineered to work more as a team than independently. In this design, the jobs are in more of a work group in which there is constant interaction and communication being shared amongst incumbents in these jobs. Think about how even changing the physical setting of jobs to align more with this collaborative design could make a difference in how these employees interact and communicate with one another.

The Work-Cell Concept

Figure 3-6 shows the work-cell concept. In this design there is no distinction between the responsibilities and functions of each incumbent, but rather the responsibilities of these jobs are shared by the employees in the work cell. In this case, each employee has cross-functional job responsibilities and learns how to perform each job in the work cell. Specific jobs may be rotated or the responsibilities of these functions are shared in some

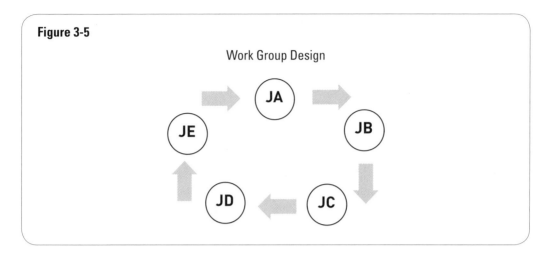

Figure 3-5

Work Group Design

other manner, usually determined by the members of the work cell. This can be a very efficient job design, as each employee can assume the responsibilities of the others at any time. Employees also gain a much better appreciation for each other's responsibilities as they perform these duties themselves. They also learn new skills and find their work more interesting and challenging as well. They begin to truly understand how each job interrelates and affects the performance of other jobs because they have performed each of these roles. They learn to appreciate how even the smallest details about how one job is performed can have great impacts on other jobs.

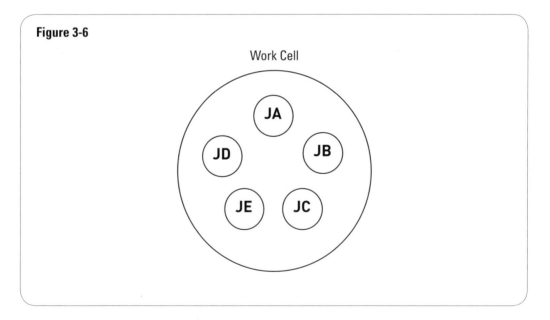

Figure 3-6

Work Cell

There can be many variations of this work-cell concept, ranging from a full integration of multiple jobs together to simply connecting them is some way, such as moving them physically closer or having them report to the same manager or supervisor. Another example might be creating an open office work environment in which by design, employees see and hear what is going on as their colleagues perform their jobs throughout the workday. In this type of workplace environment, employees are much more aware and knowledgeable about things that occur outside of their job by the very nature of the design of their work-stations. In any case, creating a work environment that encourages employees to better appreciate how their roles and those of their co-workers support one another or become cross-functional can make your workplace much more efficient and productive, as well as more interesting to your employees. Cell members are responsible for performing all of the responsibilities of the team, which includes the responsibilities of all the jobs covered by the work cell, not specific duties of one job.

Discretionary Performance

Although not every job deals directly with the customer (at least not in the sense of the buying public), staying focused on meeting the requirements of the customer is impor-tant in any job. Every function has a customer, even if it is an internal customer. *Internal customers* are those employees who receive other employees' work product in order to perform their own job. It is critical that every employee in the process understands the requirements of their internal customers and meets these requirements all of the time.

As mentioned in the introduction, there is an important concept related to employee engagement called *discretionary performance*. Discretionary performance can best be described as that extra effort employees put into their jobs to ensure they are doing everything they can to meet or exceed the requirements of their job and ultimately the customer. This discretionary effort can make all the difference when it comes to the suc-cess of most organizations, and in particular the success of their supervisor or manager.

Engaged employees put this extra effort into their job to ensure the customer's needs are met or exceeded. Think about your experiences as a customer when you purchase prod-ucts or services in your personal life. Can you tell when an employee is engaged in her job? The difference is typically how much effort and commitment that individual puts into their job. A highly engaged employee will put forth this discretionary effort to try to ensure that you are completely satisfied as a customer. A waiter or waitress may work hard to ensure that you understand what is available on the menu and may also provide prompt and courteous service. A car rental agent might ask if you need directions to where you are going and provide detailed instructions on how to get there in the most efficient manner. A clerk in a store may give you advice on the best product to purchase for your hard-earned money and explain whatever services that will be provided after the sale. A customer ser-vice representative at a call center greets each caller with enthusiasm and a willingness to provide whatever information or services the customer is hoping to receive. There are countless other examples of employees giving that extra effort, which can make such a big difference in customer satisfaction, whether direct or indirect, such as in the case where the employee never directly interacts with the customer but still influences their ultimate buying experience.

Think about what a difference this discretionary performance can make in the jobs of those employees who report to you. Imagine how this could affect the ultimate performance of your area of responsibility as a supervisor or manager. How can you help employees better understand how their job performance affects how customers feel about the entire company or organization? Sometimes employees lose sight of this; they become disengaged and rationalize or justify poor performance because of how they feel about their role in the organization. They feel alienated, unappreciated, and left out of the communication loop. As a manager, you can definitely change or influence this behavior. Think about what type of information or even experiences you can provide for your employees that help them understand how important their job is to the organization and how performing their responsibilities to the best of their ability can make a big difference.

· ·

 **WIIFM?**

1. What would be some potential benefits of helping your employees better understand how their jobs fit into the bigger picture about your function or organization?

    _____

    _____

    _____

    _____

    _____

· ·

Leadership Challenge

Just imagine if all of your employees put forth this discretionary effort in their jobs and what impact this could have on the performance of your function. What would that impact be and could it be measured? Although finding an exact measure of the effects of this discretionary performance may be difficult—if not impossible—to quantify, you should still be able to envision what its effects might be in the operation or function that you manage. Think about what some of these differences might be as a result. For example, if you supervise employees who provide service directly to customers or the buying public, list the potential benefits to this discretionary performance directed toward meeting or exceeding the customers' expectations. Or if you supervise employees in an office environment, what would the benefits be if the employees put that discretionary effort in to ensure they perform to the highest standards possible in their jobs? In other words, what are the benefits gained from filling that gap between an employee who only minimally performs his job and an employee who expends the discretionary effort to perform at an excellent level?

List below the impact difference this could have and the results which could be achieved. In the first column, list an example of a basic requirement of someone who reports to you. In the second column, list what would be an example of this employee putting forth that discretionary effort to perform this requirement of the job at a higher level. In the last column, list the potential benefits which could be gained as a result of this discretionary performance.

Discretionary Performance Impact Analysis

Meeting Requirements of Job	Discretionary Performance	Gains/Benefits of Discretionary Performance

Leader Action Planner

1. Think about how you can help your employees better understand just how important their jobs are to the end product or service of your organization. What impact could this potentially have on their performance and discretionary effort, and how can you show them this? List some of these engagement tips below.

   _____

   _____

   _____

2. What do you need to do to get started?

   _____

   _____

   _____

STRENGTHEN WORKING RELATIONSHIPS

Engaging employees can help strengthen working relationships in many ways. First, employees do appreciate the opportunity to get more engaged in their jobs. They want to be more involved in matters concerning their jobs and feel more respected when asked for their input and opinions. This can help strengthen the working relationships with those who report to a supervisor. The greatest demonstration of respect is often thought to be when you ask someone for his opinion on matters about his job. A supervisor will become more respected, not less, by asking people their opinions and expanding their level of involvement. By becoming more engaged, employees will gain a greater appreciation for the roles and responsibilities of others at work, including those of their supervisor. This also strengthens working relationships between employees, making the entire workplace more productive and satisfying to everyone.

The following MOTIVATE model is designed to help you encourage everyone in your organization to become more engaged:

Measure to make sure that employees understand how well your efforts to engage employees are working, and recognize progress toward these goals.

Optimize every opportunity to get employees more involved in the decision-making and problem-solving processes related to their jobs.

Talk to your employees about becoming more engaged in their jobs and your expectations of them in this new environment.

Inform employees about what is going on in the organization, not just what they have to know to do their jobs.

Visibly make changes that let employees know you are doing things differently to allow them to become more engaged in their jobs.

Accept employees' suggestions and opinions with an open mind, even if your instincts may tell you otherwise.

Tell your employees how much you appreciate their efforts and contributions.

Encourage employees to become engaged.

Think about how this model can help you as a supervisor, not only to motivate, but also to engage your employees. The model begins with establishing measures to help you better understand if your engagement efforts are successful or not. This can be achieved in many ways, including surveying your employees to measure this progress, and recognizing this progress against the goals you established for your engagement initiatives.

Next, the model guides you to optimize every opportunity that presents itself to engage employees. This is something you need to constantly be thinking about to ensure you take advantage of these opportunities. Often this involves asking yourself the question, "Is this something I should decide as the supervisor or manager, or is this something I should allow those who report to me to decide?" Think about the potential advantages to pushing these decisions down in the organization, both from a practical standpoint of having those closest to the work make decisions about their work, and by allowing employees to feel more engaged in their work.

Talking to your employees about employee engagement helps keep them focused and aware that this is part of the way the organization intends to operate. There should be no doubt in anyone's mind that this is the operating philosophy of the organization and that it is important to everyone and a key to your future success. You also need to be willing to listen to what your employees have to say about the engagement efforts currently in place, and be responsive when necessary and appropriate to make changes and improvements in the process.

Informing employees about what they need to know to be more engaged is also a critical component to the engagement process as discussed in the last chapter. It is not fair to expect someone to perform their job without all of the necessary information to be successful. This is like asking someone to install a piece of equipment without the proper tools.

Your engagement efforts should be apparent to everyone in the organization. It should be no secret that employee engagement is part of your leadership philosophy and is implemented. If you can't visibly see employee engagement in your organization, you should change the way you manage your function. Make engagement readily apparent to everyone, including those who work for you.

Accepting employees' suggestions for change can sometimes be difficult and counter to your instincts. You may feel you already have a good idea of how things should operate in your area of responsibility and be reluctant or even resistant to change. But you need to keep an open mind about change, especially any ideas suggested by your employees. Remember that they are the real experts when it comes to how their jobs should be performed and how to optimize resources. As least give them the chance to change your mind before deciding if their suggestions should be implemented.

Everyone needs to feel they are appreciated. Employees need to hear this on a regular basis, and will be more engaged if their efforts are recognized by their supervisor. Make sure that your engagement efforts include providing this recognition in as many ways as possible, including both formal and informal recognition programs. Tell your employees how much you appreciate their efforts.

Finally, you need to encourage employees to be engaged. Changing the way that everyone does their jobs can be difficult, especially when things have been done a certain way for a long time. When you encourage employees to take advantage of the engagement initiatives, it helps them make this transition, as well as shows them that you are committed to these changes.

The Role of the Team Leader

For a team to be effective, the team leader must be willing to examine her role in relation to the team. The team leader must take responsibility for ensuring that each member contributes and is productive. All team members must be highly committed and willing to take responsibility for the successful completion of the team's overall mission for success.

The members of the team should understand how employee engagement works and their responsibilities as a member of the team. Engagement is not a one-shot event, but a process of continual diagnosis, action planning, implementation, and evaluation. As the leader, you need to help team members work together toward their common objective of achieving the team's goals. This can be challenging at times, particularly when this goal is long-term or seems unachievable at times. This is when your role as the team's leader becomes even more critical. Everyone looks toward the leader for direction and even inspiration. Effective leaders keep everyone energized and focused on their goals, even during the most challenging situations.

Help the Team Get the Work Done

To get the work of the team done, the leader must ensure the following responsibilities are fulfilled:

- **Train team members to work together.** As team leader, you need to ensure your members have the necessary training to be productive members of the team. Provide any necessary instruction to ensure they have these skills—to not only perform their jobs as expected, but also to work together as a team.

- **Identify potential obstacles.** There are many potential obstacles that could interfere with the team's work. The team leader is responsible for removing as many of these obstacles as possible so the team can do their work. The team leader may need to appeal to top management of the organization to get help in dealing with these potential obstacles. The work of the team must be a priority for everyone, including the team leader, as he must also deal with potential obstacles within his control.

- **Suggest procedures or ideas for solving a problem.** The leader should help the team get started by suggesting ways the problem could be solved or addressed. The leader must find the right balance between providing guidance and direction to the team, while not being too dominating. The leader should suggest tasks and goals for the team, but not do all of the work.

- **Help get information.** Information can be critically important to solving problems in an organization, but you need to know where to find out key information. The leader needs to help the team find any necessary information to complete their tasks. The leader may need to direct team members about where to request data, how to seek relevant information, or when to study a problem and gather information for themselves.

- **Give input.** The leader should give her opinions about important team issues. Team members need this guidance to ensure they are moving in the right direction toward accomplishing their goals. At critical decision points, the team leader should suggest how the team should proceed. However, the leader still needs to allow the team to make decisions by themselves through working together to find solutions to problems. If not, the talent and experience of the team members is not being fully harnessed.

- **Help the team progress.** The leader needs to pull together related ideas of the members, restate suggestions, and offer a decision or conclusion for the team to accept or reject. The leader should elaborate, interpret, or redirect ideas into actionable steps for the members to perform. The leader should also help clarify any confusing points, providing explanations why something may not be possible and finding more acceptable alternatives when the team heads in an impractical or unacceptable direction.

- **Monitor progress.** One of the leader's most important responsibilities is to evaluate progress: set standards for team achievement; establish timetables for reaching goals and milestones; and measure and communicate the progress and results of the team.

- **Recognize and reward progress.** Most importantly, as the leader you must recognize the accomplishments of both the individuals and the team as a whole. You need to ensure that by becoming more engaged through participating on the team is a rewarding experience for your employees, one they would want to experience again in the future. This doesn't have to cost a lot of money. This recognition could be a note or letter, certificate, your personal thanks, lunch, a cup of coffee, and so on, presented to each participant at the conclusion of the team project as a gesture of your appreciation.

Help Engaged Employees Work as a Team

Another major responsibility of the leader is to help employees work together as a team. The following are ways in which the leader can achieve this important objective:

- **Encourage participation.** The leader should create an atmosphere for employees that is both receptive and responsive to the ideas of each member. One of the best ways to establish this type of engaged atmosphere is by modeling the behaviors that you expect the members of the team to adopt. As their leader, you set the tone for everyone. If you accept the ideas of all team members openly, the others will do the same. However, if you don't demonstrate and model this behavior, you can't realistically expect the team members to accept each other's ideas and potential contributions.

- **Facilitate communication.** You need to keep communication channels open between employees. If you see communication barriers happening, you should address any problems that may be contributing. You should facilitate everyone's participation by suggesting constructive ways to discuss team problems and any issues that might be developing in the team. You should encourage employees to express their feelings in an open and honest manner that is respectful of each other and appreciates that differing opinions are acceptable and even desirable for the team's progress.

- **Express the team's feelings.** A leader needs to have a sense of the feelings, mood, and relationships within the team. Sometimes it is helpful for the leader to express or summarize how employees collectively may be feeling at certain times, particularly at critical decision points. Recognizing the emotions and even frustrations that everyone may feel helps employees work through these issues in a more productive and positive manner. Sometimes sharing your own feelings with employees helps them deal with their own immediate emotions.

- **Explore differences.** When you help employees understand and accept that there will be conflicts as they work together, it reduces tensions that do arise. As the leader, you need to ensure this conflict doesn't become destructive to the team, but rather helps the team understand and explore different viewpoints of team members in a productive manner.

Dealing With Different Opinions

Differences in opinions at work are not necessarily a bad thing, despite what some people think. As we'll discuss in chapter 9, some conflict is inevitable in any situation in which people work together. Conflict can lead to a positive outcome if managed in a constructive manner, and can actually be productive at work by allowing different views. These perspectives, when expressed, can lead to the discovery of new ways of doing things, but they can become a problem if not managed well. A good measure of conflict getting out of control is if it causes people's relationships to be damaged as a result. A supervisor or coach should ensure that conflict is managed and doesn't become counterproductive at work.

Seeking Win/Win

There are four conflict strategies we will talk about:

- win/win
- win/lose
- lose/lose
- lose/win.

You probably have heard of these conflict strategies but may not have thought very much about how to achieve the optimum objective of win/win solutions as frequently as possible.

Although all four may be commonly used, some may be more counterproductive to developing and maintaining a workplace culture based on employee engagement. The other strategies are sometimes used more out of frustration than about trying to use the most effective conflict resolution strategy.

Obviously, a win/win strategy is the most desirable goal in many situations, but it may not always be possible to reach this level of conflict resolution. Always thinking in terms of win/win is difficult to do sometimes, as we are just not accustomed to adopting such a philosophy. We live in a competitive world with limited rewards reserved for those considered to be *winners* in life. Thinking again in terms of sports, the goal of every team or even individual athlete's performance is to win the competition. We reward and even revere winners and aspire to emulate their championship performance. This is a lot of mental programming we have to change as we try to create a more collaborative workplace.

To illustrate this point, try this simple exercise with a friend or colleague. Assume the classic arm-wrestling position by sitting across from one another with hands clasped and elbows on a flat stable surface. The typical goal of this exercise is to overpower the other person's effort to push his arm down opposite to his effort as he attempts to do the same to you. Thinking of a win/win solution to this exercise, this time the goal should be to see how many times during two minutes that one or the other of you can overpower the other person's strength and "win" the competition. The point is that if you go into this exercise with a win/lose mindset, you will expend all of your energy and time trying to overcome the other person's strength, limiting the number of times that you can reach this stated goal. But what if you really focused on the goal of this exercise, which was to see how many times one or the other of you could push the other's arm down? How could you collaborate to achieve a win/win solution? Obviously, if both of you allow the other to "win" by not resisting and work together as a team effort, you could achieve this goal easily and with very successful results.

Think about how this competitive mindset is followed, often on a daily basis in your workplace. There are many inherently natural conflicts that often appear everywhere at work. For example, in a manufacturing environment, there may be a competition created between production and maintenance departments. Production wants to keep running as much as possible to achieve the highest speeds and yields to meet ever-increasing productivity goals. Maintenance wants to be able to have access to the production equipment to do preventative activities that avoid downtime in the future, an important measure of their effectiveness. Obviously, both measures should be important to each group, but sometimes they are hard to see when you are in the midst of thinking about your own objectives. You are then oblivious of others' goals and how ultimately, achieving both is important to everyone.

In other examples, different departments in an organization seem to compete for limited resources such as budgets, resources, and even people. "I'm not going to let my best workers go to another part of the organization because I need them working in my department." This type of thinking may ultimately cause your organization to lose your most talented people to the real competition: those companies you compete against in the marketplace for customers.

These mindsets actually can reduce collaboration and create competition within an organization, which is definitely not in everyone's best interests. These different functions mistakenly view those they should be collaborating with as the competition. The result is a less effective operating organization.

The lose/win mindset is perhaps less common, but it is still played out with some regularity in the workplace. It is similar to the win/lose, but it is also a very counterproductive mindset and is often created unintentionally as a result of poor organizational design. If goals are set in a competitive manner in which there are by design going to be winners and losers, then people may no longer be motivated to achieve these objectives if they seem unobtainable. They will concede victory to some other group in a better position to be successful. An example of such a scenario is presented later in chapter 6.

Lose/lose situations are those in which everyone seems to have stopped trying to reach a goal or objective, again often because they are set too high or aggressively and inadvertently create such a mindset among employees. In this case, neither the employees nor the organization gains due to this defeatist attitude. An example of a lose/lose mindset is when a performance bonus or other similar reward program is set so high that employees feel they have no chance of achieving the goal, so they stop trying. Despite the lack of effectiveness of such programs motivating employees to perform at a higher level, the leadership of the organization insists on maintaining these unrealistic standards. In the end, neither the company nor the employees benefit.

As a manager or supervisor, you should constantly be thinking about what type of working environment you are creating for those who work for you. Obviously, the most productive is to have everyone who works for you working toward win/win solutions. Although it may not always seem like it, you do have more control over creating a win/win working environment, but you have to pay attention to this on a frequent basis. A good place to start looking is at your reward systems and what behaviors they actually reinforce. You may find that you are not achieving the results you expected due to the inherent design of these systems.

Designing Employee Engagement Into Your Organization

One way to establish more teamwork and employee engagement is to design it into your organization. This isn't really as hard as it might sound. If you look, you may even find that you have many competitive systems in place that actually inhibit or prevent teamwork from flourishing. For instance, in many organizations, there are contests or competitions that reward those who reach a certain goal with perks such as vacations, bonuses, awards, extra time off, and so on. The result of these winner-take-all contests is likely to be less teamwork and cooperation between groups of employees in the organization. This was obviously not the ultimate goal of the leaders who created these contests. They probably thought they could motivate everyone to perform better if they were striving to win the competition and receive the reward. Unfortunately, it doesn't always work out that way.

● ●

 **Case Study**

Managers sometimes think that setting up a competition between different parts of the organization will increase productivity of the organization as a whole by motivating employees to reach greater levels of performance. Competitive contests can be fine under some circumstances, but are not always effective in the workplace. Sometimes, they become counterproductive. At one manufacturing facility, the leadership team was searching for a way to increase productivity to reach the performance goals set by the corporate headquarters. They came up with the idea of introducing a contest with a reward for the crew with the highest level of production for the upcoming quarter. However, after a month, they found that the contest didn't reach the desired results. Looking at the production data over the last month, they saw an alarming trend. One crew was clearly ahead in production during this reporting period, but the other two crews were lagging significantly behind. The overall result was that the total production for the plant was down significantly from what it had been prior to the contest. In looking into this problem more closely, they learned that the leading crew got off to a fast start and the other crews quickly fell behind. This resulted in the lagging two crews becoming less motivated to be productive, as they felt they had no chance of winning the competition.

The plant manager learned of what was happening. He then quickly changed the rules of the contest. Instead of measuring the production of each crew, the manager changed the criteria to measure the productivity of the entire plant for each day. Under these new rules, everyone had a stake in the performance of each crew's performance. Employees on different crews became interested in the productivity numbers of the other crews and offered encouragement, support, and even suggestions to each other to increase productivity. The overall result of the revised rules was increased plant productivity by the end of the quarter, which had been the ultimate goal of the contest in the first place.

Systems design can have a great deal of influence on the amount of teamwork and engagement that exists in an organization. Reviewing your current organization and systems design to see where teamwork is being limited or even inhibited can help you achieve greater employee engagement. Take a close look at the systems and organizational structure currently in place in your organization. Are they supportive, or do they discourage teamwork in your workplace?

. . . .

 **WIIFM?**

1. Think about what some of the many advantages could be if your employees could work better and more effectively as a team and as engaged employees. What might be some of the advantages and gains that can help you become a better manager?

    _____

    _____

    _____

    _____

ENGAGEMENT TIPS

- Motivate employees to become engaged. Provide the resources and support needed for employees to feel like you want them to share ideas about their work.

- Help your employees learn to work together as a team to get the work done. Find out what might be interfering with teamwork in your organization, and take action to correct these problems. Talk to your employees about teamwork and get their ideas for how it can be improved in your organization.

- Understand that as a leader, you are an important part of the teamwork in your work group or areas of responsibility. You need to set the stage for employee engagement to exist. When you see employees struggling to work together, you need to help them overcome these obstacles and achieve the synergy that teamwork can create in your organization.

- Consider providing some kind of teamwork training or exercises for your employees to learn just how important teamwork is in your workplace.

Leadership Challenge

Think about a situation in which you had to deal with employees with differing opinions or points of view.

1. How effectively do you feel you managed this situation, and what strategy did you end up using?

   _____

   _____

   _____

2. How might you have handled this situation more effectively, and how might the results have turned out differently?

   _____

   _____

   _____

3. What are some opportunities for you to help your employees achieve more of a win/win result when dealing with their different opinions?

_____

_____

_____

4. What are the consequences of using a win/lose, lose/lose, or lose/win strategy to deal with disagreements with those who report to you? Do you think that ultimately these are as effective as strategies that strive to get as close as possible to win/win solutions, and why?

_____

_____

_____

• •

Leader Action Planner

1. How can you help employees work better together as a team and build stronger working relationships?

_____

_____

_____

2. How can you get started?

_____

_____

_____

CREATE MORE DEDICATED AND COMMITTED EMPLOYEES

Many employees simply come into work each day and just put in their time. This is not to say that they don't take pride in their job or do good work, but many times their heart just isn't in it. There are many reasons why this occurs, but it is often because they feel they are not given the opportunity to contribute. Or, they feel if they try to contribute, their efforts will not be taken seriously. Employee engagement programs address both of these problems by ensuring employees have the opportunity to be heard and know that what they have to contribute will be acknowledged. Employees will be much more dedicated and committed to doing the best job possible in this type of work environment than in one where they feel they are not acknowledged. The key is providing employees the opportunity to give input into decisions, problem solving, and process improvements in their workplace.

Consider the following sequence of changes in employees' overall engagement with their jobs:

Involvement $\longrightarrow$ Commitment $\longrightarrow$ Accountability

Think about what this means in terms of employee engagement. By getting employees more involved in their jobs, they will give more commitment, and then are naturally going to become more accountable for the results they achieve. There is a big difference between just performing the duties of a job and being fully committed and accountable for the results of one's work. But what makes the difference? Think about what motivates you as a supervisor to have your level of commitment to the job. What are the factors that create this type of work environment for you? How can you help those who report to you have this same sense of job ownership? Here are some ways in which you can begin to get employees more involved, committed, and accountable:

- **Allow employees to become more involved in the daily decision-making process at work.** Think about how much time you currently spend answering questions from those who report to you, when they most likely already know the answer. Many, if not most, organizations have certain hierarchies that require decisions to be reviewed on multiple levels before any final decision is made. Think about how much time and energy this potentially wastes. Consider too, that in some organizations, the person working closest to the issue is probably the best one to make such decisions. Think about how much time you could save yourself by allowing employees to make these types of decisions, and how much more involved they would feel as a result.

- **Find opportunities for employees to direct themselves.** Think about the responsibilities that your employees have in their personal lives as spouses, parents, community leaders, coaches, parishioners, and so on. They run households, civic organizations, public services, teams, and many other very responsible processes and programs. They are very capable of accepting greater levels of responsibility than you may currently be assigning them. Think about what opportunities you have to give employees more openings to direct themselves. People respond to the expectations their leaders have of them. If you expect them to be accountable for their own actions and to make more responsible decisions, it is very likely they will respond in such a manner. The point is that outside of work, these same people make very responsible decisions and self-direct all the time. They are capable of these same responsibilities at work if you give them the chance.

- **Listen to employees' ideas and provide ways that the best ones can be implemented.** Listening is an active—not passive—activity. If employees feel you are not listening to their ideas and suggestions, they will stop sharing them with you. If you show interest and become engaged in meaningful discussions with your employees about how to improve their jobs, they will continue to provide this valuable information to you. Better yet, by accepting their suggestions, you will also benefit from the results of your employees' experiences and expertise.

- **Discuss employees' goals on a regular basis and make adjustments as needed.** Everyone has goals and aspirations of some kind regardless of what position or role they hold in an organization. Providing your employees with the opportunities to tell you about their goals is important. Although you may not always be able to help employees reach all of their goals, showing interest and support will mean a great deal to them. Perhaps even if a goal or aspiration cannot be fully achieved, just being able to experience some aspects of these objectives can still be very fulfilling. Just understanding more about what those who work for you are interested in accomplishing in their career can be very enlightening and give you ideas about how to better engage these individuals.

- **Acknowledge employees' accomplishments, both big and small, on a frequent basis.** Employees often feel nobody ever recognizes the many significant things they do as they perform the duties of their jobs. Everyone wants to be acknowledged for their accomplishments, especially by their boss. This is true for both big projects as well as daily accomplishments which required extra effort and expertise. Take time to acknowledge these noteworthy accomplishments of your employees, especially when they have put forth that extra effort to get the job done correctly. This makes your employees more likely to put forth this extra effort in the future.

- **Be more visible and approachable.** Your employees want you to be physically present in the workplace. They want to be able to see and talk to you for many reasons, including asking you questions, receiving guidance, and garnering praise for the work they perform. This needs to be a priority for you in your job. Ask yourself if you currently spend enough time directly interacting with your employees as well as about the quality of the time you spend with them. You should do more than just pass through the workplace—spend time talking to your employees about what they are currently working on and the challenges they face on a daily basis performing their jobs. Think about how much better of an understanding you could gain by engaging in this regular communication with those who report to you, and the impact you could have helping your employees better perform their jobs. Even if you can't physically be in your employee's workplace on a regular basis, you still can be present virtually via Internet, web or video conferences, telephone, and so on. In this age of electronic communication, there is no reason why you can't be accessible at least virtually as a manager.

- **Provide employees with the training and tools necessary to perform their jobs to the best of their abilities.** Some positions require certain skills, and new employees in these positions would be expected to come to the company with these required skills or credentials. However, in most workplaces, the skills required to perform each job are unique to the organization or business, and new employees would not be expected to come to the job with these skills as a prerequisite. It isn't really fair to expect an employee to have these job skills if you haven't provided him with the training opportunity to learn these skills. You need to ensure you give every employee the opportunity to receive the skills training necessary to perform their job correctly. You should think of this training as an investment in your employees, which will return dividends in the future. Ask your employees what type of training they feel they need to perform their jobs better, and provide these training opportunities whenever possible.

Getting Ready for Accountability

As discussed throughout this chapter, giving employees increasing responsibility and accountability can obviously be an important part of any engagement initiative in an organization. However, everyone must be ready for this increase in responsibility and accountability, or it could actually cause employees—including supervisors and managers—to become disengaged. Giving employees responsibilities that they are not comfortable and prepared to accept is obviously not the right way to introduce employee engagement into your organization. Expecting employees to accept responsibilities before they are ready may be setting them up for failure and could be counterproductive to your employee engagement efforts. This is called reckless engagement and is the reason why many employee engagement programs fail and the sponsors of these programs become disillusioned about continuing these processes. Everyone needs to clearly understand and be ready to accept these new accountabilities. Otherwise, employees will not be completely onboard and supportive of these changes.

· ·

 Case Study

In one company, these concepts of moving accountabilities and responsibilities to lower levels of the organization had been recently introduced. An employee with many years of service, and who was highly regarded as a good worker, gave her notice that she was leaving. When asked why she was quitting she said, "Ever since I first began working for this company, I just came to work each day and did what I was told and did it to the best of my ability. I never left work thinking about what I did during my workday or worried about this place after I left the building. But now with all these new responsibilities I have been given and decisions I need to make each day, when I get home after work I find myself worrying about these decisions that I made and if I made the right decisions or not. I just want to find another job where all I have to do is put in my time again and not worry about my job when I get home at night!"

Obviously, this employee wasn't ready for this increase in responsibility and accountability that often comes with employee engagement initiatives. Part of helping employees deal with these changes in their jobs is to help them understand how to deal with this increase in accountability. Employees shouldn't feel they are being thrown into the deep end of the pool without a life preserver as a result of employee engagement. This is like having cold water splashed in your face. Instead, employee engagement should be a more gradual process, in which employees are given the opportunity to get comfortable making these types of decisions and accepting greater levels of responsibility more gradually. Again, it isn't fair to expect any employee to perform a job or accept responsibilities that they haven't been given the opportunity to learn how to perform.

The same is also true for those in supervisor roles when it comes to employee engagement. Employee engagement not only changes the roles of those who are being engaged, but also those who supervise these employees. Everyone's jobs are affected when it comes to employee engagement.

Sometimes organizations focus only on a particular department, or function, or level of the organization as they begin to introduce the concepts of employee engagement into their workplaces. This limited focus can make other groups or parts of the organization feel left out, ignored, or even less important. You should think about how everyone can potentially be affected by employee engagement including supervisors, managers, and even top management. Everyone's roles may potentially be changed as a result of greater employee engagement in the organization, and they need to be prepared for these changes.

Employee Engagement Leadership Model

Getting employees more involved in their jobs may require some fundamental changes in the way you manage others. Making this transition may not always be easy, but it can significantly change the roles and responsibilities of everyone in the workplace, including you. These changes can affect the focus of your employees about the type of decisions they make related to their jobs and your responsibilities as their manager. As their supervisor, your focus can change from making fewer decisions about how the work is performed on a daily basis to making more decisions which could affect how the work can be better performed in the future. The following *Employee Engagement Leadership Model* shows the difference in how an engaged leader deals with the responsibilities of their role from that of a more traditional management style. Figure 5-1 shows a more traditional example of how a supervisor fulfills the responsibilities of his job.

Figure 5-1

Traditional Responsibilities of a Supervisor and Subordinates

Supervisor

- Assigns jobs.
- Sets schedules.
- Prepares plans.
- Obtains resources.
- Makes adjustments.
- Makes corrections.
- Monitors quality.
- Deals with customer issues.
- Enforces rules.

Subordinate

- Performs tasks as assigned.

In this model, the supervisor assumes responsibilities for most of the tasks that he is responsible for as part of his job to get the work done. The supervisor has primary responsibility for assigning jobs, setting the work schedules, planning how the work is to be performed, obtaining the resources needed to perform the jobs, making decisions when adjustments or changes are necessary, correcting problems before or after they have occurred, ensuring the work product or service is completed in a quality manner, dealing with any internal or external customer issues, and issuing discipline or counseling employees for problems which occur at work. The subordinate employees are assigned the work and perform their jobs essentially at the direction of the supervisor. This model allows for limited, if any, employee engagement to occur. The supervisor essentially makes all of the decisions, addresses any problems which might occur, and ensures the work is completed correctly, on time, and to the customer's satisfaction. In this model, the employee's responsibility is to follow the directions of the supervisor.

In contrast to this traditional leadership model, Figure 2 depicts the new responsibilities of an engaged leader, as well as those of the engaged employees who report to her. In this model we see very different responsibilities of both the leader and the employee. In this engaged leadership model, the supervisor is focused on a different perspective than in the traditional model. This leader's focus is much more strategic. Look at the types of initiatives on the *Engaged Leader's* list of responsibilities. Each of these responsibilities is focused on proactive choices that can help improve the work process in the future. This is how a leader can make the greatest positive impact. Instead of simply directing employees how and what to do, this leader provides support and guidance to employees and allows them to make decisions—which they are capable of making, perhaps even more so than the supervisor, because they are closer to the tasks. As an engaged manager, you still play an important role—one that's even more important than in the traditional organization.

While those who report to you are now engaged in many of the activities that formerly were your responsibilities, you are now involved in much more proactive responsibilities. You are now more forward-thinking, focused on how to develop and improve the work process. The supervisor is now engaged in activities that can improve the work process in the future, and employees are given the opportunity to do what they know best by virtue of their knowledge and expertise in their jobs. In this model, everyone's true potential is tapped into and developed. Just think how much more committed employees would be in this type of a working environment than in a traditional one. The key is to make it clear to employees why these responsibilities are shifting.

This is one of the most important principles of employee engagement: giving people a chance to contribute to their greatest potential, regardless of their level in the organization. Imagine just how much more productive *you* could be under this model. In this sense, you really are getting more players in the game. You are expanding your authority by developing others to take on a more active role in the decision-making and problem-solving process in your work environment. In this case, the more responsibility and authority to make decisions you give to others, the more you expand their potential as well as their productivity.

Figure 5-2

New Responsibilities of an Engaged Leader and Engaged Employees

Engaged Leader	Subordinate
• Provides direction.	• Plans work.
• Coordinates.	• Sets schedules.
• Supports.	• Makes adjustments.
• Enables.	• Updates plans.
• Trains.	• Makes corrections.
• Clarifies.	• Ensures quality.
• Listens.	• Makes decisions.
• Plans.	• Reports progress.
• Delegates.	• Makes commitments.
• Reinforces.	• Gives input.
• Communicates.	• Takes ownership.

Engaged Leadership

In many organizations, there are certain changes in leadership philosophies that may need to take place to create an engaged work culture and environment.

Two lists of leadership philosophies and approaches are presented below, detailing how to lead others. The first list shows a more engaged leadership style or philosophy and is more consistent with the new role of an engaged supervisor as shown in Figure 5-2. These criteria outline the type of overall working relationship and management philosophy that an engaged leader needs to foster to create an engaged workplace. Employee engagement does require a new philosophy and a different approach to supervision.

For a more engaged leadership approach, include more:

- trust
- openness
- ownership
- versatility
- influence
- action.

Employee engagement is all about trusting others as well as being trustworthy as a leader. This involves being more open about sharing information, as well as listening to what others have to say. Everyone must have a greater sense of ownership in their jobs and should be more accountable for the results. Employees need to be challenged to accept more responsibility for those aspects of their jobs, as they are the experts in how to best perform the job. Influence should be based on knowledge, not just position or power. Those with the greatest knowledge and expertise rather than "position power" should be the ones who take the most appropriate action to ensure the job and operation performs to its greatest potential.

Employee engagement should also bring less of the following:

- control
- channels
- routine
- position power
- analysis
- bureaucracy.

Employee engagement should lead to fewer unnecessary controls in place. There should be less red tape and fewer channels that employees have to go through to perform their jobs correctly and to the best of their abilities. Employees should not feel like they are just putting in time at work, and instead should feel involved and engaged in their jobs. Position power shouldn't be the only influence in the organization; experience and expertise should be more important in decision making. There should be less unnecessary analysis to make the right decision, particularly when the answers are obvious to everyone. There also needs to be less bureaucracy that often causes too many of these channels and approval levels to make the right decisions. As a supervisor, it should be part of your role and responsibilities to help remove as many of these barriers to employee engagement as possible. You will be amazed at the results this simple model of engaged coaching can achieve by simply allowing employees to do what they do best—their jobs.

One of the most important guiding principles of employee engagement is the advantage of getting multiple perspectives to any decision or challenge you as a leader may face in your role. As the supervisor, you may be seeing only part of a problem. The solution may be more apparent to those closest to the actual work. As discussed previously, others may be in better positions to find the best and most practical solution to the problem. But you also can get a broader, more multifaceted approach to the problem by thinking about more solutions at once. Then you can incorporate multiple perspectives, and can come at the problem with more force and ingenuity. This is how employee engagement can really begin to help you do your job better. Asking the question, "What do you think?" to those who work for you can be one of the most important questions you can ask of your employees. This question not only can result in better solutions to work problems and efficiencies—it incorporates employees more into the team and helps them become much more engaged in their jobs.

 **Case Study**

James Robertson was in charge of a crew of cable service installers for a local media service provider in a growing metropolitan market. James had begun his career with the company five years earlier as an installer, before he was given the opportunity to move into a supervisory role. He had only been a supervisor a few months. When offered the job, he had underestimated how difficult it would be to make decisions affecting the work of others, and also he underestimated what it would be like to now supervise employees who previously had been his peers. He thought that since he knew the duties of the jobs by coming fresh from performing them, it would be easier for him to be a new supervisor. James found that moving up into a leadership role proved a much greater challenge than he had imagined.

One of the first differences he saw between these two roles was the level of dedication and commitment that employees had concerning their jobs. He even saw a difference in his own dedication from when he was an installer to now as a supervisor. Obviously, he would not have been promoted into a supervisory role if he hadn't demonstrated a high level of commitment to his first job with the company, but he did see a significant difference in the way he viewed his new role in the organization. This was also a concern for the management of the company, who noticed this apparent lack of commitment on the part of the installers, based on the number of growing service customer complaints lately. They had hoped that promoting James into a leadership role would improve the quality of service customers received, but the number of complaints seemed to increase despite his firsthand knowledge of the jobs he supervised. In fact, the opposite of what they wanted was occurring.

This was obviously a concern for James as well, who was increasingly frustrated as he tried to address this problem, and found himself working more hours each week and spending less time at home with his wife and kids. He was wondering what he had gotten himself into by accepting this supervisory position, and if it was really worth all the problems it seemed to bring into his life at the time. Curiously, the problem was that the installers did not feel James understood them or what was important to them.

James wasn't oblivious to these feelings of his crew, because several of his former co-workers were honest with him about the poor impression they had of him as a supervisor. He could also sense the growing resentment amongst this group who previously had a great working relationship with him as a co-worker. Now, they treated him as if he had gone to the "dark side" somehow when he entered management. As he sat in his office looking glumly at the latest performance report for his group, he knew he was going to receive another call from his boss about the continuing decrease in the number of installations and increasing number of customer complaints for the past month. "How am I going to turn this problem around?" he wondered, as he prepared for more pressure from his boss to come up with a solution. He knew his boss wanted a resolution quickly, which meant another long workday and less time with his family that evening.

As he drove home in the darkness that night, something one of his crew members said to him earlier in the day was beginning to resonate as he thought about this problem. Sarah, one of the best installers on the crew and someone James always had a good rapport with in the past, was very candid with him about how he was now perceived as a leader. She said the general consensus about him within the crew was that he had changed since he became a supervisor, and now he was just like all the rest of the bosses they had in the past—only concerned about making the company money and not concerned about them.

The crew was especially disappointed in him because they had such high hopes that finally they were going to have a supervisor who would truly understand and care about their needs for the difficult jobs they had to perform as cable installers in the field. Sarah also shared that in her opinion, the installers were becoming increasingly disengaged. They felt that if James wasn't going to support and care about their interests, then nobody would, and this negatively affected their morale and motivation on the job. Sarah went on to explain that it wasn't that they didn't want to do a good job. But they felt that if the company wasn't going to support them by enabling them to provide the best possible service to customers, then there wasn't much they could do to maintain this level of quality service on their own. In essence, they had stopped trying to do the best job they could for their customers, and were doing whatever they were told and little else.

After another restless night, James got to work the next morning thinking very seriously about what Sarah had shared with him the day before. He had realized that stepping up into a leadership role isn't always easy or popular, and sometimes you have to make difficult decisions that not everyone will like. But the points Sarah shared with him were different. Employees need to believe their supervisor supports them by providing the resources they need to perform their jobs correctly. He was beginning to realize that in the relatively short period of time since he became a supervisor, he had lost sight of what was important to those who now reported to him. He was just so focused on what was most important to him now as a supervisor that he was not paying enough attention to the needs of the installers. He remembered a presentation he had heard at a recent leadership conference he attended shortly after moving into his supervisory role. It was called the *Management/Employee Issues Matrix*, which he found in the materials he brought back from the conference.

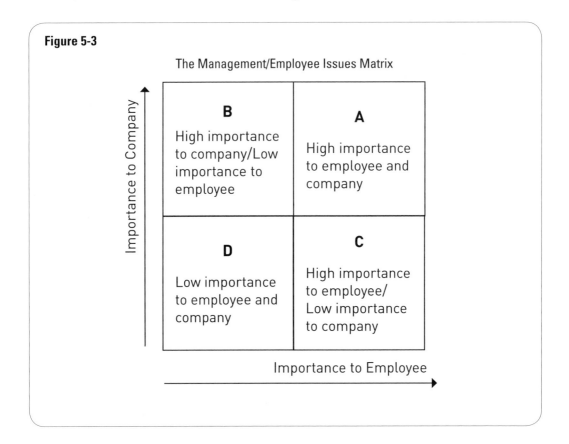

Figure 5-3

The Management/Employee Issues Matrix

As the instructor had explained during the program, on the matrix are two continuums, the vertical indicating from low to high those things that are most important to the company. This is what supervisors and managers typically focus on as they perform their jobs. These are normally the management performance metrics they are measured against, such as sales, quality, productivity, cost reduction, and so on. The horizontal continuum consists of items most important to the employee. These are things employees are generally concerned about on a daily basis, and they determine to a great extent how satisfied employees are with performing their jobs. These factors might include such things as work schedules, training, equipment, and—in the case of the installers—such things as the number of installations expected during a workday. Recognition for doing a good job by their supervisor would also be high on the list of those job factors most important to employees.

As illustrated on the matrix, Quadrant A includes factors of high importance to both the company and employees. Quadrant B includes factors of high importance to the company but of low importance to employees. Quadrant C includes factors of high importance to employees but of lower importance to the company. Quadrant D includes factors of relatively low importance to both the company and the employee.

James sat at his desk and thought about what would fit into each of these quadrants in his situation. He thought about some obvious Quadrant A factors, such as the continued success of the company and the job security this provided, the company's emphasis on its safety program to prevent injuries on the job, and the price of the company's stock (as each employee was provided shares as part of their 401K retirement program). Next, he thought hard about Quadrant B issues, which he realized would include the things he had been spending the majority of his time working on in his new role as a supervisor. These Quadrant B factors for James included such things as increasing the number of installations completed each month, efficiency ratings of the installers, measuring time of each installation, and customer satisfaction survey results.

Quadrant C issues were easy for James to identify, because it hadn't been that long ago that he was an installer himself. He remembered just how important it was to him to be given installation schedules with locations close to one another, or at least schedules sequenced in a logical order, so he wouldn't have to be constantly crisscrossing town to get from one home to another and wasting time in the process. He also remembered how important it was to have the right tools on his truck to perform his job correctly, which wasn't always the case, because there was a constant shortage of installation tools available; installers would tend to take them off their trucks to ensure they would have them for the next day's schedule. He remembered trying to convince his supervisor at the time, without success, of the need to allow installers to drive the same truck each day so they could be responsible for an inventory of tools and installation equipment of their own, as well as the cleanliness and maintenance of the truck. Thinking about these Quadrant C issues was really bringing him back to what it was like to be an installer. He realized the day-to-day problems his employees faced and how important these issues were to them.

Finally, he thought about Quadrant D issues that no one was particularly interested in, but that still received some amount of attention. In this case, James thought it was a warranty program the company had introduced a few years ago, which the installers were supposed to offer to the customer, providing coverage against any type of service problems with their cable during the next 12 months. The program never really took off, because the company already provided continued service for most problems customers might experience with their cable service, and this extra expense never seemed justified. However, the installers were still expected to present this warranty offer to each customer at the end of the service visit, even though virtually no customers were ever interested. Also, the company did not expect to receive many acceptances of this service, and they did not hold anyone accountable for the number of warranty service sales made each month.

However, since becoming a supervisor, James had been continually surprised by the many emails he received from the customer service department at the home office about this warranty program. These emails emphasized that he ensure installers offered it to each customer. They routinely did as requested, but no one ever asked how many of the warranties were being purchased. The program seemed like such a waste of time and effort on everyone's part, including the home office, except for those working in that one department who were doing what they thought they were supposed to do to keep interest in this program, but without much enthusiasm or even interest on their part. James always said if he ever got into a managerial role he would try to do something about this waste of installers' time and effort. He suddenly understood that his employees were still waiting for him to make good on this promise. He realized that he needed to address this issue with his manager, but he also knew he had a more urgent issue to address.

James realized the problem was that he had lost sight of these Quadrant C issues and he had become focused more on Quadrant B issues since becoming a supervisor. It also occurred to him that one of the reasons why he had been selected for this supervisory role was that he was able to relate to the problems installers faced.

James asked all of his crew of installers to come to a meeting that morning before they went out on service calls. He began by asking them about ideas they had to improve their performance as a team and about any issues they experienced and how they could be addressed. The installers looked at each other, a bit surprised. When James was first promoted to manager, this was the type of leadership they expected. Then, as Sarah had told James, they became disappointed when he focused on the same things their previous bosses had focused on in the past. This was a welcomed approach, and one that they were very happy to see from James.

During the meeting there was a great exchange of ideas and action plans, which were all focused on not only addressing the needs of the installers, but ultimately the quality of service their customers received. James agreed to allow each installer to keep the same truck each day, as well as to make available other resources they needed to perform their jobs to the best of their abilities. The installers also asked James if anything could be done about the requirement to present the warranty offer to each customer, which no one ever accepted, and he committed to bringing this up to his supervisor the next time they met. James left the meeting finally feeling that he was moving in the right direction as a supervisor for the first time since accepting his new role.

 **WIIFM?**

1. What could be some advantages for you when you give those who report to you greater accountability and decision-making authority in their jobs? What opportunities could this create for you to focus on more strategic issues in the future?

_____

_____

_____

_____

_____

⚙ Leadership Challenge

1. Think about how getting your employees more involved and accountable for their work can increase their feeling of commitment and dedication to their jobs. What are some opportunities to give your employees greater levels of accountability in their work and jobs?

   _____

   _____

   _____

2. What specific decisions could you allow your employees to make that you are currently responsible for making?

   _____

   _____

   _____

3. How might giving your employees greater levels of responsibility and authority give them a greater accountability in the way they perform their jobs?

   _____

   _____

   _____

💡 Leader Action Planner

1. What are some of the first things you need to do to give your employees this greater level of responsibility and decision making in their jobs?

   _____

   _____

2. How can you get started?

   _____

   _____

DEVELOP YOUR EMPLOYEES' STRENGTHS AND ABILITIES

Think about the potential of those who work for you, and ask yourself if you as a leader are fully developing this talent. Creating a workplace supportive of employee engagement helps enable you as a manager to more fully tap into and develop the strengths and abilities of your employees. Your employees are the greatest resource you have, and more fully utilizing their talents will empower you to fulfill your responsibilities more effectively.

You should think about training and developing your employees as an investment, not just an expense, the same as you would for any other business expenditure. The problem is that often when there is a need to reduce costs, training and development activities are the first things to be cut. This is a mistake and should be avoided whenever possible. However, measuring return-on-investment (ROI) is usually difficult when it comes to training and development of your employees. Sometimes the results of training are harder to quantify in the same way as, say, indexes measuring efficiencies after installing a new piece of equipment. However, you need to know if you are getting a return on this investment in your employee's capabilities.

To begin, let's think about your employees from a different perspective. Usually you think about your employees' abilities in relation to their work performance on their current job. This is what we would typically call *performance*. Performance, accordingly, is measured in many ways, but most frequently by some form of annual performance evaluation process linked to a specific rating scale developed or adapted by the organization. It is likely your organization has such an evaluation system. Identifying your best employees is usually an output of this process, with those receiving the highest ratings considered the top performers in your work group or organization. These are the employees who often receive the most opportunities to develop their skills and abilities, not only to perform their current jobs, but also for future positions.

However, there is another dimension of performance that isn't always so easily identified or measured. This is an employee's *potential* to perform at a higher level than his current position. Looking at the model shown in Figure 6-1, you see *Performance* on the horizontal axis and *Potential* on the vertical axis. Performance in this case would be a measure of how well an employee performs her job. Potential is what we believe this individual's ability is to perform at a higher level or in a more responsible position. This potential could be

Figure 6-1

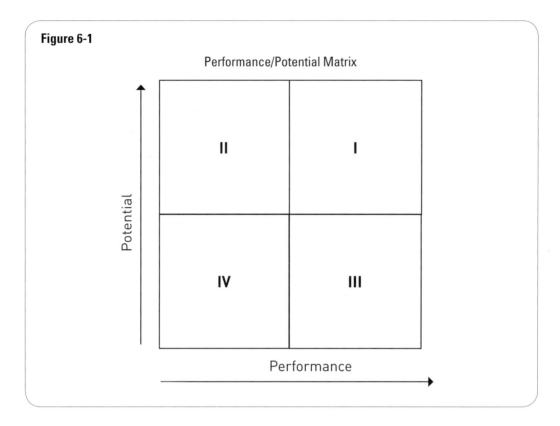

Performance/Potential Matrix

evaluated based on many traits, skills, characteristics, abilities, talents, training, and so on, observed by you and others.

Let's look first at Quadrant I of this model. In this case, the employee would be evaluated as both performing her current job at a high performance level and having the potential of being promoted to a higher position in the future. You should certainly invest in this person's development for the future.

Next, look at Quadrant II—this is someone who may not currently be performing at a high level in his current position, but who does have the potential to do so in the future. If you have someone working for you who would fall into this quadrant, you should ask yourself more about this individual. First, you should wonder why this individual is not motivated to perform to his potential currently. What is it about this position that inhibits this person's performance? Is it something that could be addressed and corrected? Or, think about if this person is in the right role or one that challenges this employee to perform at a higher level. Clearly, for someone who falls into this quadrant, something needs to be discovered and changed to enable him to perform to his potential. This could include a reassignment to a different (more appropriate) position for him. This person may also be in a new position and has not yet had the chance to develop the skills necessary for performing the position at a higher level.

Quadrant III employees are performing their current responsibilities at a higher level, but for some reason, they are not considered as having the potential to assume greater responsibilities in the future. This could be for many reasons: the individual's motivation level, stage in his career, or lack of any other positions that would be more suitable for this person. It is also possible that this person's high performance is a function of the length of time he has been in his current role, where he has had the advantage of time and experience to be able to perform his current job at such a high level. Moving someone in this quadrant to another position may only cause him to fall into Quadrant IV on this model.

Finally, Quadrant IV employees are not currently performing their jobs at the highest level on your organization's performance rating scale, nor do they have the potential to move to a more responsible position. You may need to either focus on providing these employees opportunities to acquire the skills and knowledge to perform their jobs at a higher level or just accept the level of their current performance. However, it is important to keep in mind that in most organizations, the majority of employees will most likely fall into this quadrant for various reasons. Their current performance level may be fully acceptable, but they are not considered as the highest potential candidates for the top positions in your organization in the future. If you looked at a bell curve of the performance level of all of the employees in your organization, you would most likely find that up to 70 percent of your employees fall into this quadrant. However, this is the group who has the most to gain from your employee engagement initiatives. They are the ones who typically feel forgotten and overlooked in favor of those with high potential as they move up in the organization. Many, if not most, of these employees may not have the same opportunities as your high-potential employees. This group needs to have the opportunities to be more engaged in their jobs and to be recognized for performing their jobs better. They want to be heard and feel that their opinions matter. They want to be engaged in not only their jobs but also in making a greater contribution to the success of the organization.

Figure 6-2

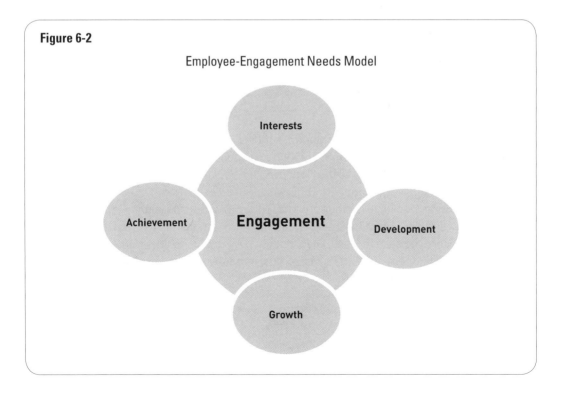

Employee-Engagement Needs Model

In this model, the basic needs of employees to become more engaged are presented. Employee engagement focuses on employees' interests, development, growth, and achievement. All of these needs must be addressed, or you will have something missing in your employees' expectations and experiences with their jobs. This process naturally begins with employees' career *interests*, which represent their hopes and dreams for the future. To achieve these interests in their futures, employees must be provided with the *development* opportunities to achieve their goals. These developmental activities lead to employees' *growth* and eventual *achievement* of their career goals and aspirations. When there is a lack of alignment with these four types of employee needs, then something is wrong and you will have a dissatisfied employee. Multiple different scenarios will follow when this misalignment occurs. If there are other career opportunities available outside the organization, the employee will be much more likely to leave the organization to seek this alignment. Or, if there are not other career opportunities, then the employee will stay with your organization but may become actively disengaged. Addressing this alignment can make a tremendous difference in the engagement level of your employees.

Everyone can't be a superstar, but each employee has something unique to contribute and inherently has the desire to do so if given the opportunity. It is up to you as their manager to find the key to helping each person who works for you to reach her potential as an employee. This model can help you understand what might need to be addressed for your employees to become truly engaged.

The Real Experts

Employee engagement is based on the belief that decisions are best made by those with the greatest understanding and knowledge about the issues at hand. Again, most often this is the person working on the job, who is closest to the problem based on his knowledge and expertise. The employee working on the job is the real expert based on his experience in the position (assuming the employee has performed the job for enough time to gain this expertise). Why wouldn't you go to this expert when making decisions or working on a project, as this person has more expertise and experience than anyone else in the organization for that specific task?

Getting the right people working on the right things is critically important to the success of any endeavor and it is important to creating and supporting employee engagement. Supervisors should ensure they have the right people who are the most knowledgeable about the problem working on the problem. Otherwise, you can experience *blind obedience*. This is when employees do exactly as they are told. This may sound like a good thing, but it isn't necessarily desirable. Sometimes employees follow directions or instructions from their boss while performing certain tasks, even though they know it isn't the right solution to that problem. Obviously, the result can be disastrous, as seen in the following example.

> *Manager:* I thought you would be completed with that project by now, but it seems like you haven't even started. What's the problem?
>
> *Employee:* Remember, you told me to wait until you gave me the go-ahead to begin. I never heard from you, so I waited to start working on this project.
>
> *Manager:* OK, I do remember now. I must have gotten busy and forgotten to follow up with you. I wanted you to get started some time ago and now we are going to be way behind. I wish you had let me know that you were still waiting to hear from me to get started.
>
> *Employee:* Sorry. I wasn't sure what I was supposed to do.
>
> *Manager:* I understand. Next time I will give you better instructions what to do if you find yourself in this situation again in the future. But for now, let's get you started on this project and see if there is something we can do to get you caught up.
>
> *Employee:* OK, just let me know what you want me to do.

Clearly, you don't want employees to feel unable to speak up or let you know when they are waiting for you to give them further instructions to perform their jobs. In the above example, perhaps it would have been better to empower the employee to make the decision when to begin the project based on her own judgment instead of making this decision depending on the manager. Employees need to be able to contribute their ideas and expertise while performing their jobs and also while making decisions about their jobs—especially when feedback from the manager overrides the successful performance of the job. Teach your employees to think more broadly about how their work is successful, and make that the primary concern. Creating a work environment based on engagement prevents this type of problem from happening. So you need to create a working environment where an employee feels her opinions matter and that she will be listened to when sharing critical information needed to resolve a problem.

Helping Employees Contribute

Employees on all levels do want to contribute to the success of their organization. Part of your role is to create a work climate that supports employees' feelings that they can contribute to the overall success of the organization.

People appreciate being asked for advice, and they like to participate in the decision-making process, particularly when they are knowledgeable and have expertise in a specific job. They want to contribute and play an important role in the success of the team. However, not everyone will demonstrate this willingness to contribute to the team in the same way. As a supervisor, one of your most important responsibilities is to find the key to getting this commitment from each employee. Employees need to be given the chance to contribute to a team in different ways. Often it is a matter of finding the right task or role for each employee, and when you get people and tasks lined up correctly, you can tap into the true power of employee engagement. This brief dialog between a manager and an employee illustrates high engagement.

> *Manager:* I really liked the initiative you took to ensure that the customer was satisfied with the service you provided to her. I heard you offer additional assistance and go beyond what you were required to do to help her. This makes a big difference to our customers and it is what makes them keep giving us their business.
>
> *Robert:* Thank you. I enjoy helping people and ensuring that they are satisfied with our service. I always think about the way I would want to be treated when purchasing something, and try to provide that same level of service to our customers.
>
> *Manager:* I like your attitude and commitment to the customer. Do you have any ideas how we could continue to improve our customer service?
>
> *Robert:* As a matter of fact, I do have a number of ideas that I believe could make a big difference in the level of customer satisfaction that we are able to achieve.
>
> *Manager:* Great! Let's schedule some time together later today so I can hear about your ideas. How about 2:00 p.m.?
>
> *Robert:* That would work for me. I look forward to sharing my ideas with you then.

Think about an experience you may have had when finding the key to an employee's real interest and talents at work. Did it help motivate that individual to contribute to the success of the work group or organization? You may be able to do this more in the future as part of engaging employees in your workplace.

Ask/Tell Approaches to Communication

You need to have different supervisory approaches to communication when dealing with employees depending on their levels of experience and job mastery. The degree that a supervisor engages in either *asking* or *telling* employees about performing their jobs should be based on employees' experience and skill level, as well as their level of comfort performing the job or task, as shown in Figure 6-3.

Different employees obviously have different needs when it comes to the type of interaction time they need or even want to have with their supervisor. The basic rule should be that the less job mastery an employee has, the more supervisory time should be spent helping her perform the job correctly. Conversely, the greater the skill mastery, the less supervisory time you need to spend explaining or telling the employee about how to perform the job. But spend more time asking for her input about how the job could be performed better. However, following this does not mean that time spent communicating and building better working relationships isn't still important for any employee, regardless of job skill and experience. This will always be important under any circumstances. There may still be times when a supervisor will need to direct an employee on any changes

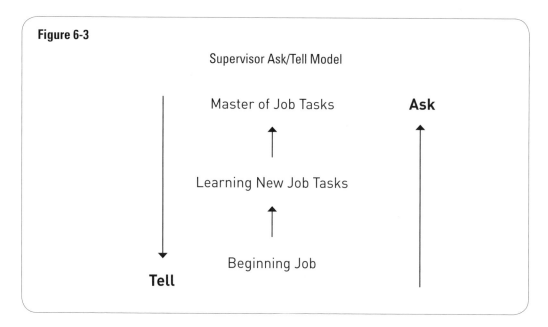

Figure 6-3

Supervisor Ask/Tell Model

or new initiatives. Also, there will be more management direction if any experienced employee's performance begins to slip below acceptable levels.

Reasons Why Employees Don't Perform to Their Potential

There are many possible reasons for employees not performing to their potential on their jobs. Many believe it is often a matter of employee motivation that causes most performance problems at work. However, the concepts of employee engagement focus on the workplace environment as well as employee motivation. In most cases, employees respond positively to a work environment that provides the opportunity for them to engage in their work each day—they want to do a good job. Since employee motivation is affected by other factors in the environment, let's take a look at some of these factors and how they can be avoided.

Lack of Communication

Employees need to clearly understand what is expected of them by their supervisor. Most employees, if asked, will say they are not always clear on what their supervisor does expect of them. They need to receive clear individual communication and direction from their supervisor that pertains specifically to them and how they are expected to perform their job. Part of this communication should include both formal and informal feedback about how they are performing their job. This feedback needs to be the proper balance of reinforcement and opportunities for improvement, again specifically tailored to the employee's performance. This communication also needs to be clear and consistent. When there is a lack of consistency, employees receive a mixed message that only confuses them.

In Figure 6-4, differing perceptions of a job are illustrated, showing that supervisors and employees don't always think similarly about what is most important for the job. Sometimes, there can be significant gaps in these expectations, and if there is very little overlap of commonalities with these perceptions, it can be a major problem. This problem is much more likely to exist if there hasn't been dialog between the supervisor and the employee about these expectations. Obviously, both the supervisor and the employee need to agree about what is most important in the performance of the job so that their expectations can match. As a manager, you need to ensure that those who report to you clearly understand what you expect from them as priorities when they perform their jobs. If the employee doesn't understand your priorities, then neither of your expectations about the way the job is performed will be met.

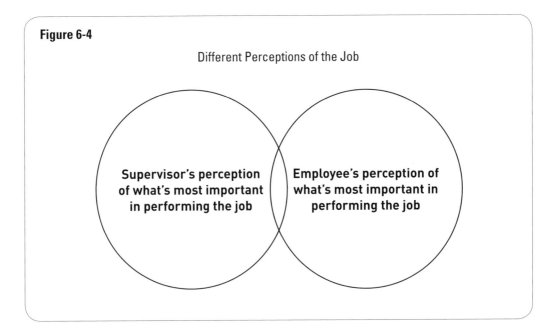

Figure 6-4

Different Perceptions of the Job

Supervisor's perception of what's most important in performing the job

Employee's perception of what's most important in performing the job

Lack of Conditions

This can include employees having the proper training or instruction to be able to perform the job, having the necessary tools or resources to do the job, or even having enough time to perform the job properly.

Lack of Consequences

There need to be both positive and negative consequences, as appropriate, based on an employee's job performance. Too often, there are no consequences associated with an employee's job performance. This can give an employee the false impression that no one cares how he performs his job. This is counterintuitive to what employee engagement is all about. Employees need to understand the importance of their job as it relates to other employees' jobs. Even the smallest of details can be extremely important when it comes to meeting the goals of the organization as a whole, and each employee's contribution is important.

Becoming a more effective communicator is a worthwhile goal of anyone in a leadership position today. So much of creating and maintaining a workplace supportive of employee engagement is based on establishing good communication. Engaged employees will learn to depend on you to provide them with candid and timely information on all matters related to their jobs and the entire organization. Meeting this challenge is one of your most important responsibilities as a supervisor of engaged employees.

Setting Performance Standards

You need to set and communicate the performance standards for employees to reach, and not allow poor performance to go unchallenged or unaddressed. As a manager, you have the right to expect nothing less than excellent performance from employees. There are two basic rules about managing performance:

- Always expect excellent performance.
- Never let poor work go unnoticed or performance issues go unchallenged.

If you let poor work go unchallenged, this sends a bad message to other employees, as well as to the poor performer. The unintended message is that this level of poor performance is acceptable. The good performers who work hard to meet your expectations become frustrated, and this affects employee morale as well as employee engagement. The morale has a direct relationship on engagement in this case.

The Five-Step Performance Correction Process

Your approach to performance problems has a lot to do with how successful you are in resolving them. This is especially true when coaching a new employee about her job or teaching her a different task or skill. The correct approach to use was explained in the Ask/Tell model presented earlier. By following this five-step performance correction process, you can ensure you address the issue in the most proactive and supportive manner possible.

1. **Observe:** Supervisor states what she observed: In this case, the work wasn't completed according to the most current specifications.

> *Supervisor:* "Henry, I don't think that you are following the most recent specifications for completing that job. These were updated last month and I thought that I had communicated these changes to everyone in the department."

2. **Discuss:** Listen to the reason the employee gives you for not getting the work completed according to the new specifications.

> *Henry:* "Now that you mention it, I do remember you reviewing the new procedures at our last monthly meeting. There have just been so many changes lately that I have been having trouble keeping up with all of them. Sorry."

3. **Correct:** Tell the employee what you want him to do the next time he is faced with a similar problem.

> *Supervisor:* "I understand. There have been a lot of changes in procedures recently and it is hard to keep track of all of them sometimes. We keep these changes updated on the system with the most recent ones listed in chronological order. It might be helpful if you logged in to that site on a regular basis to help you keep up with these changes, especially now."

4. **Advise:** Give the employee additional advice on how to correct the problem next time, in case he runs into a similar problem in the future.

> *Supervisor:* "I know that several others in our department take a quick look at this list every morning before they begin their assignments to remind them of any changes which may have been implemented that may not have been communicated otherwise. I have found a few situations like this and have been logging into the site every morning for that reason. It has really helped me stay on top of things."

5. **Confirm:** Make sure the employee clearly understands what you expect him to do in a similar situation.

> *Supervisor:* "We all need to make sure that we are up to date on the most recent procedure changes so I would appreciate if you could check this site on a regular basis. It is up to you how frequently you check to make sure you are up to date, as long as you are sure you are aware of the most recent changes."
>
> *Henry:* "OK, that sounds like a good idea. I will start logging in on a regular basis, probably every day like you do. Thanks for the advice."
>
> *Supervisor:* "I think you will find that once you make it a part of your routine, it really is helpful and not that hard to do. Let me know how this works for you."

You should use this five-step approach in a manner and style that is most comfortable to you. It doesn't matter if you follow these steps exactly, but it's most important that you make clear what you expect from employees, and then follow up to ensure everyone understands these expectations.

Engaged Leaders Still Enforce the Rules

Employee engagement doesn't mean there are no rules or consequences for not following the procedures in an organization. Employees who follow the rules will become upset if they perceive others are allowed to break the rules without any consequence. Part of becoming an engaged leader is to ensure the rules of the organization are followed by everyone, and when necessary, you take the appropriate actions to correct problems with any nonconformance issues.

• •

WIIFM?

1. What could be some advantages of providing these opportunities for your employees to reach their potential on their jobs? How would this help you to achieve your own personal and career goals?

    _____

    _____

    _____

• •

Leadership Challenge

Think about how much of your employees' potential you may be currently realizing as they perform their jobs.

1. What would be some opportunities to develop these employees to reach their potential?

    _____

    _____

    _____

2. What types of development, training, or other opportunities exist that could help develop this potential in your employees?

    _____

    _____

    _____

3. What might be some benefits to your work group or organization by tapping into this potential of your employees?

    _____

    _____

    _____

4. How can you ensure that the performance standards of your organization are being met and if not, what actions should you take to ensure they are met?

_____

_____

_____

• •

Leader Action Planner

1. What are some of the first things you need to do to help your employees reach their greatest potential on their jobs?

_____

_____

_____

2. How can you get started?

_____

_____

_____

LEAD TO BETTER, MORE PRACTICAL SOLUTIONS TO PROBLEMS

Many times organizations spend millions of dollars trying to find ways to address problems, which, if they had only asked those working closest to the problems, could have been resolved more practically and quickly. By engaging employees, managers provide them with more opportunities to share their experiences and expertise acquired by virtue of performing their jobs.

Turn Good Ideas Into Great Ideas

There are typically many good ideas about how to improve an operation of an organization, but finding *great* ideas can be a much bigger challenge and much more infrequent in most organizations. Engaging your employees may be one of the best ways to turn good ideas into great ideas. Many problems show up later on in the development of a plan or project unexpectedly. This occurs frequently because the plan for moving ahead was not fully vetted by the right stakeholders in the process. Again, those working closest to the root causes of problems are typically in the best position to provide advice on how to proceed and avoid costly problems later on. But you have to ask for their opinions and provide them the opportunity to become engaged. Expanding their perspective of their own function or operation can give them additional opportunities to provide their expert advice. Engaged employees typically can give you practical and workable solutions at a fraction of the price that outside experts may be able to provide you. The most expensive lesson organizations often learn is when they hear their employees tell their supervisors, "I could have told you that wasn't going to work if only you had asked me!"

Engaged employees can often solve problems or provide better advice than anyone else, regardless of his position. This collective experience and knowledge of an engaged team is a powerful force. Harnessing this powerful force to help deal with the organization's most challenging problems is your responsibility as leader of the team. Leadership needs to understand that all the brains are not always at the top of the organization. Getting the right people working on the right things is critically important to the success of any endeavor.

Creating teams of engaged employees can become one of your most powerful resources you have as a manager. As leader of the team, one of your most important responsibilities is to find the key to getting this commitment from each member. Every employee brings his own unique skills, talents, experiences, intuitions, and so on to the team. Employee engagement creates *synergy*, which is the blending of different human skills, talents, and experience to produce a total effect greater than the sum of the individual team members' skills, talents, and experiences.

Phrases That Kill Good Ideas

There are certain things people sometimes say that actually kill or seriously wound what could otherwise have been good ideas. These words can be very disengaging to employees. You might consider posting this list of *killer phrases* to help your team avoid saying these things. The list would also help everyone recognize when these or similar comments are made that could impede the creativity and progress of the team. Next to each of these killer phrases are more positive statements, which would be much more engaging.

Killer Phrases	Positive Statements
Don't be ridiculous.	That might not be a bad idea.
It'll cost too much.	We shouldn't just look at costs, but return on this investment.
That's not my responsibility.	How can I help?
I don't have time to talk about it.	Could we set another time to discuss this topic?
We have never done it before.	It's time that we try new things.
If it isn't broken, why fix it?	We need to be proactive before problems occur.
We're not ready for that.	We need to be prepared for change.
You can't teach an old dog new tricks.	It is never too late to learn something new.
We've tried that before.	We need to be open to new ways of doing things.
It can't be done.	We won't know if it will work or not until we try.
It's too big of a change.	Maybe we need to introduce this change in phases.
It's not our problem.	If it is a problem for one part of the organization, it affects all of us.
Let's get back to reality.	Anything is possible. We need to think differently.
You're getting ahead of yourself.	I like the way you think ahead.
It's not in our budget.	We need to see if this can be added to the budget.
Let's wait to decide.	Let's see if we can make a decision based on what we know now.
That doesn't really apply to us.	We may have to deal with this at a future time.
We have done alright without it.	What could be the potential benefits?
It won't work in our business.	We need to try this in our business to see if it will work.

Work Toward Consensus

Consensus is different from agreement. Agreement implies that everyone feels the same way about something. This is not an easy objective to achieve and might not be possible in many situations. People often have very strong beliefs and convictions on just about any topic or problem they may face as members of a team. Reaching consensus is a much more realistic objective. The concept of consensus is very important in teamwork. Teams must strive to reach consensus on whatever they decide should be the best course of action to take or decision to make. Consensus means that everyone involved agrees that he or she can support the idea of a path forward for the team even though it may not have been their idea or preferred plan going forward. Everyone on the team must be committed to work toward consensus. Consensus sounds something like this: "Although this isn't what I had initially thought the team should do, I do agree to support what the team has decided and will work toward making this decision successful."

Think about how much more effectively your employees can work together with this definition of consensus in mind, and help them work toward this goal whenever they work together as a team. Think about what often happens when someone's idea or input is not accepted by the team. The result is often that person becomes disengaged and no longer works productively as a member of the team. Remind team members about this concept of consensus, and how working with this mindset can result in a much more productive and engaged workforce. This way, everyone feels a sense of commitment and ownership for the success of the team's plan.

Tap Into the Knowledge of Your Employees

People often disparage the number of meetings that are typically held in most organizations and the amount of time invested (and often wasted) in them. But calling a meeting to get different perspectives on an issue is still a good one, and it is important to your success in implementing an employee engagement initiative. The problem with most meetings is that they are not led effectively. As an engaged leader, you need to ensure the meetings you hold with your employees as part of your engagement process are conducted in the most effective manner possible. Under these circumstances, your team meetings will be productive and successful.

Lead Effective Meetings

An important responsibility of a leader is to arrange for the members to meet regularly and work together as a team to share and develop new ideas. As stated above, being able to lead effective team meetings is critically important to the success of any team. Team meetings are potentially more productive when members can be physically present and meet face-to-face. However, with the technology available today, meetings can be held in a virtual environment. Meetings can be conducted via teleconferences, webinars, interactive computers, and in many other ways enabled by the technology available.

Regardless if the meeting is held face to face or in a virtual environment, there are certain responsibilities that you as the team leader need to keep in mind to ensure the meeting is as productive as possible. Because meetings are typically such an integral part of the engagement process, if the team's meetings are not run well, the success of the process could be jeopardized. The following are basic team meeting fundamentals that can help you run effective and productive meetings in the future. Following these team meeting fundamentals will greatly enhance the success of your employee engagement efforts.

Plan the Meeting

Team meeting fundamentals start with planning. An effective meeting requires pre-planning, particularly setting up an agenda and sharing it with everyone beforehand. You should determine the purpose of the meeting and what you expect to accomplish during the time you spend with the team. A good way to do this is to list the things you want to accomplish during the meeting and then create an agenda listing these objectives in logical order. Determine how much time you believe should be allotted for each agenda item and set time limits for discussion on each agenda item. Be sure to include any prework or preparation that's expected, as well as any other special instructions that participants may need about attending the meeting. Decide who should be invited to the meeting, including any special guests or subject matter experts outside of your team that could add to the value of the meeting.

Lead the Meeting

Meetings need to be led and organized to be effective. This is typically the responsibility of the team leader. However, you might decide to delegate this responsibility to another team member. If you do, remember as meeting leader that you are still ultimately responsible for the success of the meeting. Make sure that those who you may assign responsibility to during the meeting perform their roles and tasks in an effective manner. These roles could include scribe, who is responsible for ensuring that meeting minutes are taken and distributed to each participant afterward. This ensures there is a written record of the meeting afterward and follow-up agenda items are captured. You may also choose to assign a timekeeper to monitor amount of time spent on each agenda item and to alert the team leader when the meeting is getting off schedule.

As the leader, you should establish from the very beginning the expectation that participants are required to attend all team meetings unless excused, and they should be on time for the meetings. Everyone at work is very busy and their time is valuable. You should also ensure the meeting ends on time. Again, people have other responsibilities that they must attend to during their workday, and you shouldn't exceed the allotted time you asked them to dedicate to the meeting.

Effective meetings require a certain amount of discipline, including staying focused on the agenda. Everyone needs to stay focused on the decisions that need to be made as part of the process. During the meeting, as a group, you should agree on what to accomplish for each agenda item. Give everyone the opportunity to provide her input into the discussion.

While discussing each agenda item, focus on how to resolve specific problems or how to reach the goals. Ideally there should be numerous alternatives discussed about each problem, and you should get a consensus about the best possible alternatives to follow. The meeting leader should constantly move the group toward decisions on key issues without dominating the discussions.

Brainstorming

An effective way to get team members thinking creatively is brainstorming. Brainstorming allows each employee to contribute her ideas in a free-flowing format. At least initially, there should be no critiquing of ideas, regardless of how outlandish or ridiculous they might sound. Some of the greatest discoveries started out seeming impossible, but with some refinement, they became great ideas.

Rules for brainstorming include:

- The topic for brainstorming should be as specific as possible.
- Each team member in rotation is asked to volunteer a single idea. This continues until all ideas have been exhausted.
- Each member offers one idea per turn.
- Strive for a quantity of ideas.
- Not everyone has an idea during each rotation. When this occurs, team members should be allowed to just say "pass."
- Evaluation of any kind is not permitted.
- Freewheeling is encouraged and welcomed, even the absurd or ridiculous.
- The more ideas, the better.
- Combinations of, elaborations on, and improvements of ideas are encouraged to produce better, more creative solutions.
- No idea should be treated as stupid.
- No criticism of an idea is allowed.
- Good-natured laughter is encouraged.
- Exaggeration should be encouraged.
- All ideas must be listed.

Multi-Voting

Once you are sure that everyone's ideas and creativity has been fully tapped and exhausted, the next step is to review the ideas or suggestions. Even during this step in the process you need to withhold judgment of ideas. You never know when even the most outrageous idea might not really be so crazy with a slight modification.

Using a multi-voting process, you can reduce the brainstorming list to those that the team feels are most useful or appropriate. Multi-voting involves simply asking participants in the brainstorming exercise to vote (usually by a show of hands) which brainstorming ideas should continue to be considered, until you have only one left. Multi-voting rules should be kept simple. You could give each team member only a certain amount of votes to expedite the process. For example, if you have a brainstorming list of 50 ideas, each team member could be given five votes to choose which ideas he feels are best. The brainstorming idea that receives the most votes will then become the decision of the team.

Multi-voting example: Each employee was allowed three votes to select the project that he felt the team should work on. The following were the voting results of the team members as they multi-voted for the team's project:

Project Suggestion	Votes
Reduce scrape rates.	I I
Reduce purchasing costs.	I I
Decrease processing time.	I I I I
Begin recycling project.	I I I
Improve departmental communication.	I

As a result of the multi-voting, the team selected *decrease processing time* for their project.

Create a Project Plan

Creating a project plan can help a team stay focused on their goals and deliverables. A project plan creates a written record of each goal or step in the process the team has undertaken and provides for easy follow-up on progress toward completion of the project's steps and goals. The following is an example of a project plan template that could be utilized by your teams to keep everyone focused on the goals and progress of the team. It is also important to keep your project plan constantly updated and available to all team members.

Conclude the Meeting

As the meeting moves toward completion of the agenda items, it is important to conclude in an effective manner and on time. This is a good time to review what was agreed upon during the meeting, and also a good time to clarify and summarize assignments. Take the following steps during the conclusion of the meeting:

- Confirm what agreements have been made.
- Agree on action steps that need to be taken.
- Delegate responsibility and set deadlines for completion.
- Determine how and when to evaluate the effectiveness of the actions to be taken.
- Establish who will report back the results of the actions at the next meeting.

Figure 7-1

Your Project Plan

Goal	Team Member(s) Responsible	Deliverable	Measure	Due Date	Status

Critique the Meeting

Before the meeting ends, you might find it helpful to take a few moments to ask each meeting participant how he felt about the meeting and ask for suggestions to improve future meetings. This gives participants the opportunity to provide input and helps make future meetings better.

Follow Up on the Meeting

There are typically numerous items that need follow-up attention after the meeting is over. It is critically important that any assignments made during the meeting be completed—especially before the next meeting. If these assignments are not completed, the progress of the entire project and team's work will be delayed. As team leader, you will find it beneficial to check on each team member's progress on any action items assigned to him during the time period between team meetings. You can do this by simply inquiring on his progress or asking if he needs any assistance in completing the assignments. This shows you are interested in the employee, plus, your attention highlights the importance of the team member's assignment in reaching the goals of the team.

The discussion might go something like this:

Team Leader: "Before we end the meeting, does anyone have any critiques or suggestions about this meeting?"

Team Member: "I think it would be better if we reported on our assignments first thing during the meeting instead of making this the last agenda item. It seems like the way we are doing it now, there isn't enough time for everyone to get a chance to explain all about what they are doing."

Team Leader: "OK, that sounds like a very good suggestion. I will put this first on the agenda for our next meeting if that's OK with everyone. Thanks for your suggestion."

It is also important that you ensure the minutes from the meeting are written up and distributed to each member, as well as to any other individual in the organization who would have interest in the team's progress.

As soon as the last meeting is completed, it is time to begin planning the next meeting. Some things you should consider for the next team meeting are:

- What action items need to be addressed when the team meets again?
- What follow-up actions need to take place?
- What information needs to be reported back?
- What progress needs to be tracked and reported?

You should develop the next meeting agenda with these questions in mind. And the meeting planning process continues, with you notifying team members in advance of the next time and place.

 **WIIFM?**

1. What would be some of the advantages to you as a supervisor if you led more effective meetings in the future?

   _____

   _____

   _____

Leadership Challenge

1. Think about how much of your employees' time is invested in meetings. Are you getting the best return for this investment of time? How can you make these meetings more productive?

_____

_____

_____

_____

2. How could you get your employees more engaged in making these meetings more effective?

_____

_____

_____

3. What might be some of the benefits to your work group or organization by improving the effectiveness of these meetings?

_____

_____

_____

4. How could helping your employees work toward consensus as they work together help you achieve your engagement objectives?

_____

_____

_____

5. How could you ensure that your organization is designed to support employee engagement so that there aren't counterproductive processes in place that inhibit engagement?

_____

_____

_____

• •

Leader Action Planner

1. What are some of the first things you need to do to tap into your employees' talents and abilities to increase the level of employee engagement in your organization?

   _____

   _____

   _____

2. How can you get started?

   _____

   _____

   _____

CREATE BETTER COMMUNICATION

C ommunication is the key to solving virtually every problem at work. But this is still a "get what you give" world, and communication is a two-way street—you have to share information to receive information. Employee engagement improves communication between employees, as they are encouraged to share more information with one another. A critically important part of creating a culture of employee engagement is to improve communication on all levels in your organization. Information is a powerful force in any organization. Exchanging information is important to creating and maintaining an engaged workplace and workforce. Opening up these channels of communication helps keep everyone better informed and therefore better able to perform their jobs.

Employee engagement involves creating a work culture and environment in which employees on all levels feel that they are important and contributing members of the organization. Engaged employees want to do a better job and make that extra effort to ensure they meet others' expectations, including the customer. Perhaps most importantly, engaged employees feel that based on their experience and expertise on their jobs, they have something important to say and others, especially their supervisor, will listen to them. So you need to establish an open two-way dialog with employees where there is a free exchange of thoughts and ideas on how to continually improve to meet the goals of the organization. This might be called *talking engagement*.

The Importance of Establishing Good Communication

Communication is a powerful force in any workplace and organization. Communication is either the cause or the solution of virtually every problem you deal with in your leadership role at work. For example, can you think of a situation at work in which communication (on some level) was not the root cause of that problem? If you think about this question carefully, you will most likely find that communication was at the root cause of just about every problem you deal with and has been the solution to most problems as well. This proves just how important establishing better communication can be in your working relationships, and why focusing on this important factor is a worthwhile endeavor. This ultimately allows a leader to be better informed as a result of exchanging information.

Communication affects everything that happens in organizations. Communication is one of the organization's greatest strengths or one of its greatest weaknesses. This is also true for supervisors. A supervisor's communication skills can make a big difference in how effectively she performs her job. The good news is that anyone can improve their communication skills. You don't have to be a great orator or public speaker, but you simply need to try to be a better communicator. Communication is much more of an art than a science. There is no absolute right or wrong way to communicate effectively. What is most important is that you communicate in a manner and style most comfortable and effective for you.

Leadership Communication

As a manager, you play an important role in how your employees think about their jobs in relation to the rest of the organization. What type of information you communicate to those who report to you can make a big difference in how they are able to relate to the rest of the organization. If they receive little or no information about other parts of the organization outside of their own job function, then they won't be able to relate to anything other than their own job responsibilities. However, if you keep your employees well informed about what's happening in other functions of the organization, they will have more interest and understanding about how their jobs are connected to the rest of the organization.

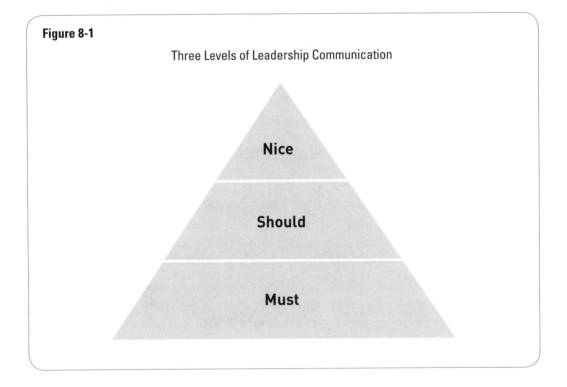

Figure 8-1

Three Levels of Leadership Communication

Nice

Should

Must

In Figure 8-1, the three levels of leadership communication describe the broad levels of communication you share with your employees. The communication that employees "must" know includes the most basic information such as the location of their work station, the time they are expected to be at work, and the tasks they are to perform. Typically, this type of communication is shared with employees as much as possible, because they cannot perform their jobs without this information.

The next level in this model is information that employees "should" receive, but may not always. This information typically relates to employees' jobs, but is not absolutely necessary for them to have to perform their jobs. This might include what other employees are working on, what changes may be planned in the future that could affect their jobs, or feedback about the quality of their work. It could also include providing employees with greater access to other parts of the organization, or even the jobs literally next door to their job station. It could involve cross-training or job-shadowing opportunities. These are like creating *adventures at work*, where employees are given the opportunity to explore other parts outside of their everyday work world.

The top level of this model represents the type of information that is simply "nice" to know. This is information that may have nothing to do with one's job but still is news about the organization as a whole. These types of communication include business updates, business forecasts, leadership strategy, sales presentations, budgetary information, competitor information, financial reports, long-term company vision, market studies, customer surveys, and so on. Often, it is believed that there could be risks in sharing too much of this type of information with everyone in the workforce, but this is something you should really think about and decide on the risks compared to the benefits. Sometimes this information provides a scope of the organization, and that allows them to become more engaged by identifying more where they fit in the whole scheme of things.

At what level do you believe you are presently communicating to your employees? Certainly you are providing "must" level communication, or they wouldn't be able to perform their jobs. But how often do you provide "should" and "nice" level communication to those who report to you? Think about how these types of communication could influence your employees' performance in the future. For example, how could helping your employees better understand more about other employees' jobs help them perform their own better? How would this help them appreciate how their job interrelates with the jobs of other employees, and what affect could this have on their own performance? How could sharing "nice" to know information help make employees feel more a part of the bigger organization? When you share information, it builds trust and camaraderie, because as a manager, it shows you trust them with confidential information. What influence might this type of information have on how employees perform their jobs? Would employees appreciate hearing information that is "nice" to know? Perhaps most importantly, how could sharing this type of information with your employees on all levels of the organization help you meet the requirements of your customers?

For example, one employee was asked about something relating to his job that wasn't going to happen until sometime in the future. He said, "Every day when I come to work I only receive just enough information to be able to perform my job for the day, nothing more. I never know what I am going to be doing the next day or anytime in the future until that time comes and I get my job instructions for that day."

Obviously, this employee was only getting "must" level communication, if that. How engaged do you think this employee was, and how much did he feel his supervisor trusted him? Employees do want to receive information about their jobs and the organization in general, even if it doesn't directly affect them. Creating an engaged workplace is built on sharing this type of information with employees. This makes everyone feel more a part of the entire team and lets them know that you care enough to ensure they receive this nice-to-know information. Also, sometimes nice-to-know information actually becomes "should" or even "must" know information.

Finally, what about information that an employee should *not* know as it relates to this communication model? By communicating consistently on the "nice" level, employees will be much more understanding when told that certain information can't be shared with them. So, if you have created this higher level of trust in your communication with employees, they will be more accepting if you find yourself in a position when you do know something they may have asked about, but you are unable to discuss it at this time.

Communicating Assignments

An important part of a supervisor's communication is how effectively he explains assignments to employees. The successful completion of the assignment may largely depend on how well it was communicated to the employee who performs the task.

The following checklist will help ensure that you are communicating assignments most effectively:

- Make your expectations exactly clear when giving an assignment.
- Make sure that employees have all the information needed to complete the assignment.
- Give employees a chance to ask for clarification or questions about assignments.
- Explain why it is important to complete the assignment correctly.
- Tell employees what others will be working on that relates to the assignment.
- Check on employees after giving an assignment to see if they have any other questions.
- Ask employees for any feedback on the instructions, such as "Do you understand what to do based on these instructions?"
- Ask employees for their input about how the assignment should be completed before beginning.
- Listen to any suggestions employees may have about how the assignment could be completed more effectively.
- Ask employees if they are comfortable with being able to complete the assignment.

Engaged Supervisor's Communication Model

This model (see Figure 8-2) illustrates how you become a more effective communicator with your employees who report to you. Although this may seem like a cumbersome process to go through at first, the best communicators practice this model in some manner in all of their communication, although perhaps not as formally as this model, instead following the basic principles.

Look at the first step in this process, in which the supervisor sends a message. Even at this early step, many problems can occur. For instance, the message may not be clearly communicated by the supervisor. This could be a function of the supervisor's communication skills or even the effort that this person puts forth to communicate clearly.

The employee receives the message and both hears and responds to the message. There can be problems with both. The employee may not be able to clearly hear the message for multiple reasons, including other distracting sounds, or competition for his attention by others. One part that's usually overlooked is having the employee respond to the message. Of course, this can't be done if he doesn't hear the message or chooses not to respond. In either case, the message would end at this point in the communication process, as is often the case.

The supervisor clarifies anything the employee may have misinterpreted in the message. This is another chance to make sure the manager's message was heard correctly.

The employee confirms that he now understands the message, and the process is complete.

When you put the concepts of this model into action, you should personalize and tailor them to your individual personality and style. You don't have to follow this model strictly every time you communicate with others, but practice these essential concepts. Especially keep these in mind when sharing important information to those who report to you, as illustrated in the case study later in this chapter.

When you stay in the communication process longer, you confirm that everyone has the same understanding. This is critically important for supervisors who want to improve their communication with employees.

Figure 8-2

Engaged Supervisor's Communication Model

1. Supervisor sends message.

2. Employee hears and responds.

3. Supervisor clarifies any misunderstanding of the message.

4. Employee confirms understanding of the message.

Listening

Most people would say they are not really good listeners, but listening is an important part of any job, and especially a supervisor's job. Learning to be a better listener is certainly a worthwhile endeavor for you to pursue, particularly if your goal is to create a more engaged workplace. Those who report to you want you to be a good listener. They undoubtedly feel they have important things to say that are important to them and want your undivided attention at these critical times. The following listening tips can help you become a better listener.

LISTENING TIPS

- Paraphrase the message to the speaker in order to confirm your understanding.
  Repeating what you believe to be the meaning of the message to the sender can help clarify the actual intended meaning if the message is misunderstood.

- Repeat the message to help you remember what was said.
  Repeat out loud what you just heard to retain the information longer.

- Probe for missing information.
  Probing for information allows you to ensure that you receive all the information you need to act, as well as keeps you actively involved in the communication process.

- Remember the important points of the message for future application.
  Focusing on those most important points of the communication can help you focus on precisely the parts of the message you need the most.

- Act upon the message as necessary.
  The best time to respond to the message is instantly if possible, before you get distracted with other competing tasks. Do it now, before you forget!

Silent Messages

Sometimes when you say nothing, you are unknowingly saying a great deal. Taking no action or not addressing a problem could deliver an unintended message to employees. Many times when we think we are not communicating, we are actually sending a very strong message. This is particularly true for supervisors. For instance, say you see inappropriate or unproductive behaviors being displayed by an employee in your presence and you say or do nothing to correct this situation. The perceived message is that you condone this type of inappropriate behavior or that you just don't care. This is the wrong message and doesn't promote what any manager wants or expects from employees.

If you see inappropriate behaviors on the job, you should not be silent and you should take immediate corrective action.

 **Case Study**

Leon Anderson had been in management for almost 30 years, and he was one of the most respected leaders in the company, in part because he was such a good communicator. Leon wasn't a great public speaker, and he didn't typically go around saying profound statements, but everyone always left any discussion with him clearly understanding what he expected of them. Here's what Leon did to achieve this level of communication: Every time he gave instructions to one of his employees, he asked that person to repeat the instructions back to him. His employees quickly learned they needed to pay very close attention to everything Leon said, because he would test them on their understanding of the assignment. After receiving his instructions, employees would often ask him for clarification on the assignment. Leon always had the full attention of his employees every time he communicated with them. Just saying that you understood him wasn't good enough for Leon—you had to demonstrate this understanding.

It was really amazing that Leon was able to repeat this process with just about everyone he talked to at work. Even to someone in upper levels of management, he would typically end discussions by asking the person with whom he was talking to summarize what they had just agreed to so everyone had a clear understanding of the conversation. In this way he made everyone he talked to become a better listener. Leon made everyone he came in contact with a better overall communicator as a result.

WIIFM?

1. What might be some of the benefits to your work group or organization if you communicated at this higher level?

    _____

    _____

    _____

2. What are some ways in which you could become a better listener at work, especially with those who report to you? How could improving your listening skills help make you a more effective leader?

    _____

    _____

    _____

    _____

    _____

COMMUNICATION TIPS

- You can learn a great deal communicating with those who report to you, especially if there is a two-way exchange of information.

- Really listening to what your employees are saying can help you better understand the key to helping them become more engaged. They will share this information with you, but you have to listen to what they are saying.

- Communicating at a higher level with your direct reports helps build leadership credibility and trust.

- Don't always assume that you are being understood by everyone you communicate with at work. Staying in the communication longer to ensure that you are understood (and that you understand others) is important in your role as a supervisor or manager.

 Leadership Challenge

1. Think about how you communicate with those who report to you. Do you believe you are an effective communicator? Think about how your approach to communication with your employees affects how they perform their jobs.

   _____
   _____
   _____

2. Think about a problem or issue that recently occurred in your work group in which a lack of communication was the most likely root cause. Think about how more effective communication could have made a positive difference in this situation. What could you do next time you are faced with similar circumstances to communicate better?

   _____
   _____
   _____

3. At what level on the communication pyramid are you presently sharing information with your direct reports?

   _____
   _____
   _____

4. What opportunities exist for you to share more information on a "nice" to know basis with your direct reports, and how could this help them feel more engaged as employees in the organization?

_____

_____

_____

● ●

Leader Action Planner

1. What are some of the first things you need to do to become a more effective communicator as a manager?

_____

_____

_____

2. How can you get started?

_____

_____

_____

REDUCE STRESS
IN THE WORKPLACE

Our world today is filled with stress as we strive to be successful in both our personal and work lives. Reducing the stress which employees experience at work is one of the many benefits of introducing employee engagement in an organization. People tend to feel especially stressed by those things they have little or no control over. Part of engaging employees is to give them more involvement—and ultimately control—over the problem-solving and decision-making processes in their jobs. This ultimately can reduce the amount of stress they have at work, creating a more relaxed and productive workplace. Building this less stressful and more productive workplace environment will be a positive reflection of a manager's leadership, as well as having the benefit of reducing their own stress level at work.

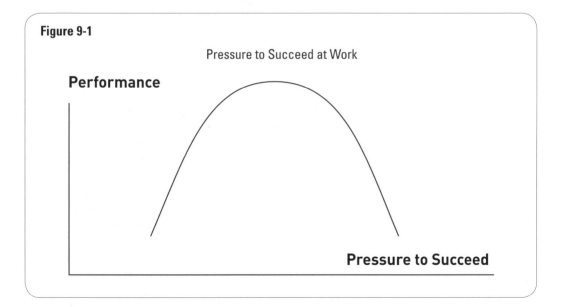

Figure 9-1

Pressure to Succeed at Work

Performance

Pressure to Succeed

Pressures to Succeed

There is no doubt that we live in a world of increasing pressure to get everything done in our busy schedules at work and at home. This pressure certainly exists in the workplace, as the demands at work to get more done with less resources increases. These pressures at work cascade down in an organization from the top to increase shareholder value in a very competitive marketplace. As a manager, it may seem that the only way you can meet these increasing demands for higher levels of performance is to put more pressure on your employees.

However, as Figure 9-1 illustrates, simply putting more pressure on employees to produce more can get to the point of diminishing returns. As you can see, putting more pressure on employees can result in higher performance, but only to a certain point. Putting too much pressure on employees can reduce performance overall, especially if you overload or burn out people in the process. This is where the concepts of employee engagement can be most beneficial.

Figure 9-1 represents the traditional way that many leaders believe is the way to get better performance from employees. However, the concepts of employee engagement suggest that you approach this challenge in a different manner. In an engaged workplace, a supervisor would be more likely to discuss the production goals the organization is hoping to achieve, and together develop a plan to achieve this objective. Just asking employees who are already working hard to work even harder is not the way to achieve such an ambitious goal. Instead of asking employees to work harder, what you should be asking them is how they can work *smarter*. Ask employees for their ideas about how to improve their performance and increase their output. This is a better strategy for achieving goals and is much more likely to be accomplished, especially over time. Employees will feel a greater sense of ownership for the established goals, and will be much more likely to work toward successfully reaching them if they are engaged in the process. They will also feel less pressured and stressed out by what they likely feel were unrealistic demands being imposed on them—without any say about those decisions.

Helping Employees Deal With Conflict

Another cause of stress in the workplace is when conflict exists between employees, or even between supervisors and employees. Conflict may sound like it is on the opposite end of the spectrum from employee engagement, but it is actually part of the process. Conflict is inevitable in any situation in which people work together. People bring many different perspectives to work, and this causes conflict. Some conflict is a natural part of working together. But conflict is not necessarily a bad thing. Conflict can help achieve better, more creative solutions to problems. It allows different perspectives to be expressed and explored by employees who work together. Better solutions are the result of beneficial conflict.

However, it needs to be managed to ensure conflict doesn't become counterproductive. It must not get to the point where it damages relationships. Learning to deal with conflict constructively is an important goal in achieving teamwork and supporting an engaged workplace. Helping employees learn to deal positively with conflict should be part of your responsibility as a leader.

A *Leadership Conflict Resolution Matrix* can help you better understand the different ways to deal with conflict at work. These strategies can help your employees work through conflict more productively.

Figure 9-2

Leadership Conflict-Resolution Matrix

+ A S S E R T I V E N E S S -			
	Reject	Confront	Collaborate
	Resist	Judge	Negotiate
	Retreat	Give In	Ignore
	- I N V O L V E M E N T +		

First, look at the indexes on both the horizontal and vertical axes. On the vertical axis is the *assertiveness* scale from low to high. This indicates the level of assertiveness one may use to deal with conflict at work. On the horizontal axis, the *involvement* scale reflects how one may deal with conflict from low to high. These nine strategies are combinations of assertiveness and involvement. For example, the *retreat* conflict strategy is lowest in both assertiveness and involvement. On the other extreme, you find *collaborate* is the highest in both assertiveness and involvement.

It is important to understand that each of these strategies can be an effective way to deal with conflict depending on the situation and circumstances. None of these strategies are necessarily right or wrong, but all may conceivably be the best strategy in a certain situation. For example, when confronted with conflict, it might be best to retreat. This would likely be the best strategy if someone is confronted by another person in an argument or potential physical altercation. However, this strategy would not be most effective in every situation. It is your job as a manager to help team members understand and learn how to use as many of these conflict management approaches as possible. This will help everyone work better together and deal constructively with conflict.

For instance, find the *reject* strategy, which is at the top of the assertiveness continuum and lowest on the involvement continuum. Rejecting an idea may not always be pleasant, but it does have the potential of resolving a conflict quickly and decisively. This may be the best strategy if given circumstances have a conflict that needs to be quickly addressed.

The *confront* strategy may also fall into the category of being unpleasant but sometimes effective as a conflict management strategy. Sometimes unaddressed issues cause conflict to continue unchecked. If you simply confront the behaviors that are causing the problem, this can resolve the conflict. Confronting conflict and its causes can sometimes be an important role of the team leader (when used at the right time and circumstance).

The *resist* strategy is another frequently used conflict strategy. This strategy is in the middle of the assertiveness continuum, which makes it more comfortable for some people. Resistance, when it comes from a leader, mostly sends the message that he is opposed to the conflict, but not yet committed to taking definitive action to address the issue. Hopefully others will get this message and end the conflict on their own. There can be different levels of resistance, ranging from passive resistance to more active resistance, which sends a stronger message from the leader.

The *ignore* strategy is also complicated, in that using this approach in the wrong situation can make it worse. However, certain circumstances require that you ignore the situation. Sometimes, letting a conflict resolve itself may be the best strategy. In some circumstances, a team leader who gets actively involved in the conflict may only make things worse. This can be especially true when two team members are having a conflict between them and you feel it is best they work out their issues themselves. However, in these circumstances, you need to keep aware of the situation and make sure that it does get resolved by itself.

The *give in* conflict strategy is low assertiveness but has high involvement, and thus may sound like a poor way to resolve conflict. However, giving in can be an effective conflict strategy, especially when the issue isn't important to the leader or team members. Sometimes we find ourselves taking a more assertive position just for the sake of argument. But if something isn't really important to you, then there isn't any sense in fighting for it, and the best thing to do is allow the other person to have her way. This is why it is on the high end of the involvement continuum, as it takes certain involvement to use this strategy in the right situation. Team leaders and team members need to recognize these situations, and give in when it makes the most sense to do so.

The *judge* conflict strategy is in the middle of the assertiveness and involvement continuums. As its name implies, this strategy involves evaluating the conflict and making some kind of determination about which side of the conflict is right and which is wrong. Judging is a frequent role for the team leader. As any good judge or arbitrator, you must remain as impartial as possible in these situations, and make decisions based solely on the facts and circumstances of the situation. You often decide according to the rules which have been established by the organization. Also, you should explain your rationale for making such judgments, because it helps those involved more readily accept your decision.

The *negotiating* conflict strategy typically involves each side giving something up to reach a compromised outcome. As the leader, you may find yourself playing the role of a mediator in a conflict situation, in which this sort of process is the best way to be fair.

Finally, the conflict strategy highest on both the assertiveness and involvement continuums is *collaborate*. When everyone collaborates, they are trying their best to find the most acceptable ways to resolve conflicts and problems at work. They are totally engaged in the conflict resolution process and are open to all suggestions to resolve any existing conflicts. Having a collaborative attitude can resolve even the most difficult conflicts that exist in the workplace. Perhaps one of the greatest advantages of creating an engaged workplace is the collaborative spirit it can create throughout the organization.

An important point to understand about these conflict strategies is that each of the responses to conflict can be an effective and appropriate way to resolve conflict within your work group, depending on the situation. One of the things you will learn as an engaged leader is that *you don't always have to be in control of every situation that may arise at work*, including conflict amongst your employees. Sometimes less is more when it comes to conflict resolution, and allowing your employees to resolve conflicts within their group on their own may be a better strategy. Using as many of these conflict strategies as possible, including those on the less assertive or involved continuum of this model, can be just as effective, if not more so, as those involving more leadership control.

Conflict Comfort Zones

Each of us has our own conflict comfort zone that we naturally gravitate toward when faced with a conflict situation. In other words, this is the way we instinctively respond to conflict. This may have a great deal to do with our own unique personality style as a leader, as we are all either more or less assertive or involved in the way we interact with others. Understanding your unique conflict comfort zone can help you better deal with conflict, which will inevitably arise in the normal course of people working together.

Think about how you typically react to conflict when you try to resolve it. Do you usually re-act in the same way (do you revert to the same conflict strategy) every time or most of the time? If you do, this is your conflict comfort zone. The problem is that this may not always be the best way to deal with conflict as a leader. For example, there may be times when you use a confrontational style of conflict management when a cooperative approach might be more effective, or vice versa. Learning to use all of these conflict strategies as a leader can help make you a much more effective conflict manager.

 **Case Study**

Hillary Wellington had become frustrated that her work group seemed to be in a constant state of conflict with one other. Members of her team were in her office on a daily basis, complaining about what she perceived to be petty squabbles between each other. Most of these issues seemed to be about either workload issues or personality clashes. Hillary never imagined when she first moved into a leadership role many years ago that her greatest challenge would be trying to resolve her employees' arguments amongst themselves. Hillary, by nature, did not have an aggressive personality, and admittedly disliked conflict. She usually tried to avoid it whenever possible.

Then one morning her boss called her into his office to discuss her work group's performance, which had been steadily decreasing over the past few months. He wanted to know if Hillary knew why this was happening. As Hillary sat in her boss's office, she thought about all the conflict her team had experienced lately, and she realized this was probably why their group was declining in performance. She knew it was her responsibility to resolve these conflicts.

"I think I know what the problem is and I will take care of it," Hillary said. Her boss looked bewildered. Realizing that he wanted some explanation about the cause of this problem and her plan to address it, she explained. "There have been many disagreements among my team members recently, which I have not done a good job in addressing and bringing to some kind of resolution. The performance numbers you just showed me tell me that most if not all of this problem is based on this conflict in my group. I believe that if I can address these conflicts more assertively, you will see a significant improvement in our performance."

Hillary remembered learning about the *Leadership Conflict Resolution Matrix* during a webinar she recently participated in, and so she found a copy of the handouts she had downloaded from the presentation. She looked at the matrix and saw that her natural conflict style was on the low end of both the assertiveness and involvement continuums. She also realized that her responses to the ongoing conflict were largely responsible for her group's performance problems. Ignoring these conflicts and hoping they would vanish was definitely not working, and she needed to act to change this situation immediately.

Hillary spent some time studying the *Leadership Conflict Matrix* and thought about which specific strategies she had used when members of her team came to her with their conflicts. She judged herself as relying too heavily—in fact, exclusively—on the retreat, resist, and give-in strategies. She remembered the webinar facilitator advising that each of these strategies could be effective, depending on the situation. Hillary remembered feeling somewhat relieved to learn that less aggressive conflict strategies like her own natural style could be effective when she was first presented this matrix. But she was coming to the realization that not moving away from your natural conflict comfort zone when the situation dictated it necessary was a big mistake.

As Hillary studied the matrix, she began to think of multiple different conflicts between her employees that had been brought to her attention. She had either ignored or only passively provided input or guidance to the involved employees. She thought about other ways in which she could have been more assertive to allow her team to move beyond these disagreements and focus more on their work. For instance, she remembered one situation where an employee was not following the proper work procedures and others complained to her about the problems this caused. Hillary encouraged these employees to work out this issue themselves, hoping they would work toward a cooperative solution. This did not resolve the problem, and only seemed to make matters worse. She realized that she should have confronted the situation and addressed this problem directly with the employee who did not follow proper procedures. Hillary was learning that you can't just hope or expect employees to work cooperatively together—sometimes you have to take a more assertive role in resolving issues that naturally arise between employees at work.

The next time Hillary met with her boss to discuss her work group performance, the numbers were much improved. Her boss was obviously pleased with this turnaround, and asked her how she was able to achieve such remarkable results in a short period of time. Hillary answered, "It's just a matter of knowing when to get more involved and assertive, and when to take a more passive role as a leader. It's all a matter of timing!"

Dealing With Upset Employees

One of the most challenging situations a supervisor faces is of dealing with an upset employee. Regardless of the reason the person might be upset, there are many skills that can effectively manage these types of situations.

The first thing to keep in mind is that the employee is most likely in a highly emotional state of mind and may say and react in ways he would not normally under different circumstances. Keep in mind that this employee will soon return to his normal state of mind and you don't want to do or say things that will ultimately damage your working relationship with that person. How you deal with this situation can make or break not only your working relationship with that person, but also his level of engagement at work going forward. Obviously, this is an important moment in your working relationship with an employee who is in a highly emotional state. Treating an upset employee with dignity and respect under these circumstances is of paramount importance. Part of showing respect is giving this person your attention and listening to his concerns and reasons for being upset. Providing a private location for this discussion is important to avoid other distractions taking away from the employee's issue and privacy keeping this interaction away from the attention of others. The following are tips on dealing with an upset employee:

- Let the employee vent. This can be an important part of the process of dealing with an upset employee. This is a time to listen, not to argue or present counterpoints to the employee's current concerns. The employee is probably not in a state of mind to really listen to the logic or rationale that you might present and counterpoints will only cause him to feel you are not really listening to his specific problem. What the employee is most likely trying to convey to you is how he is feeling at the moment, and if you judge these emotions with statements such as "You shouldn't feel that way," it will only appear that you don't understand the problem or don't care about his feelings.

- Don't try to problem solve too soon before you have completely heard the employee's concern or complaint. Look into each person's situation and understand the uniqueness of their situation. That is what each individual really wants you to understand under these circumstances.

- Don't immediately reject the employee's request or proposed remedy until you have had time to thoroughly investigate. Avoid making commitments either positive or negative to the employee until you are fully prepared and ready to make such a decision.

- Ask for additional information and ensure that you understand (to the employee's satisfaction by repeating your understanding of the problem to him) the problem from the employee's perspective. Remember that the problem the employee initially came to you upset about may only be a symptom of a different issue. Make sure that you truly understand the root cause of the problem before trying to address or solve the issue, or it will continue to occur in the future.

- It may be a good idea to schedule a time to talk to the employee later on if he is too emotional to have a rational discussion with you at the moment. Even if you decide to discuss the problem with the employee at the time, it may still be a good idea to have a follow-up discussion to clarify points made during your initial meeting. You may find some inconsistencies between what was initially reported to you and what you are told during subsequent discussions, so be prepared for these differences. Be careful not to bring into question someone's integrity or honesty if you hear such inconsistencies, as people often say different things once they have calmed down and are not in a highly emotional state of mind.

- Establish a timeline for following up on the employee's complaint, and if there are any changes, let the employee know. Avoid making or even inferring a decision on the complaint if you don't know for sure that it may be possible. This will only make things worse if any expectations cannot be met.

- Once you have heard everything you need to know about the employee's complaint, look into the situation to see if there is any solution or remedy to the problem. Check to see what policies or practices might be established to help resolve the problem and to see how similar situations were dealt with in the past.

- Get back to the employee as soon as possible and explain your decision (or that of others). Accept ownership for the decision and avoid passing blame for an unfavorable decision on someone else. If the decision is not favorable to the employee, explain the reason and rationale for the decision. Explain any options the employee may have to appeal the decision, such as escalating the complaint to a higher level in the organization if possible.

- Follow up on any actions that were agreed to that would be made as a result of the complaint to ensure that they are being implemented.

- Depending on the nature of the complaint, provide resources or referrals to other support systems which may be available to the employee, either within the organization, or from external resources as appropriate.

Providing Feedback to Employees

Not receiving any feedback from one's supervisor can be very stressful for many employees. Without feedback, an employee does not know whether she is meeting, exceeding, or failing a supervisor's expectations. Everyone needs to receive feedback about how they are performing their jobs. Providing feedback to employees helps them understand how they are valued by you and the organization. Many employees leave jobs because they erroneously believe their boss doesn't appreciate them, when nothing could be further from the truth.

Feedback is important in any activity we engage in, in our daily lives, or even when pursuing our favorite pastimes. What would it be like if you received no feedback when you pursued some of your favorite activities? For instance, this time instead of golfing, imagine what it would be like if a bowler received no feedback on his performance, and he wasn't allowed to keep score.

Blindfolded Bowling

What if every time a bowler threw his ball down the alley a curtain dropped, preventing him from seeing how many pins were knocked down. Say that this process was repeated during every frame of the game. How likely would it be for this bowler to have a good score? Without this performance feedback, he wouldn't know how to tell good from bad performance. How much enjoyment and satisfaction do you think this bowler would be experiencing? What if the bowler had no score during the game? Or what if the bowler's score was presented to him by the owner of the bowling alley at the end of the quarter or calendar year? How would these things affect the bowler's ability to improve his performance during this game or subsequent games?

If you are a bad bowler, you may be thinking it might be better to not see the results of your performance. But what makes bowling enjoyable and challenging, like golf as we discussed earlier, is getting feedback immediately after each action. Either the bowler sees the results of throwing the bowling ball properly or the consequences of not performing correctly. It would not do you much good during your game to receive your scores in the mail months later.

Just like the bowler, employees need immediate feedback on their performance. They need to know their score about how well they perform their jobs in real time. They also need to receive this feedback on an ongoing basis instead of just once a year. Engaged employees need to receive feedback and coaching about their performance on a regular basis.

Feedback for Continual Learning

Feedback is important to growth, development, and continual learning in life. The purpose of feedback is to promote learning and thus enhance performance. Coaching gives employees feedback and helpful suggestions that will allow them to grow and develop on their jobs. There are four levels of feedback that an employee might receive from her supervisor. Each of these four levels is better than the previous one, with the last one as the ultimate level—what you should strive for.

No Feedback

Think about some of the many problems created if an employee receives no feedback at all about her performance. Unfortunately, this is all too common in many workplaces, and often becomes the default performance feedback system.

> **The Default Performance Feedback System**
>
> "If you don't hear anything, you are doing just fine. But if you screw up, we'll let you know!"

The greatest problem with this is that employees won't know if they are performing the job correctly; they will not have any opportunity to grow if there is no feedback to direct them. Again, it simply isn't fair to hold someone accountable for things that you never discussed with her.

Only Negative Feedback

What happens if an employee only receives negative feedback? This is also a common occurrence in many workplaces. This situation creates problems, such as negatively affecting the employee's self-esteem, creating a negative work environment, lacking reinforcement to motivate the employee, and creating a poor working relationship between the employee and the supervisor. This type of work environment would most likely disengage employees.

Only Positive Feedback

What if an employee only receives positive feedback, assuming that there are negatives to be discussed? If employees don't hear about those aspects of their job performance that are lacking, they won't be able to address these problems and grow in their jobs and careers. In many ways, a manager does an employee an injustice by not communicating where the employee needs to improve and by only telling her the positives about the performance. Often, it is this type of feedback—the one that is hardest to hear—that can ultimately be the most beneficial to the employee's growth and development on the job.

Balanced Feedback

Balanced feedback, which is an appropriate amount of both positive and negative information provided to the employee, is the optimum level of feedback an employee should receive from his manager. Balanced feedback means that the person receives both positive and constructive feedback on how he can improve performance. The ratio of positive to negative should be determined by the employee's actual performance, but there should typically be much more positive than negative feedback presented to the employee. Usually an employee's strengths are first presented, and then any areas that he could improve upon should be reviewed in a constructive developmental way.

Types of Feedback

There are basically two types of feedback that an employee can receive: formal and informal. These are fully detailed below.

Formal and Informal Feedback

Formal: documented annual/semiannual performance review. Formal feedback is typically provided as part of the organization's established performance appraisal process. Formal feedback is generally given annually, sometimes with midyear update reviews. There is usually a standard form required by the organization and an evaluation system that requires supervisors to rate each employee. This rating typically determines the amount of raise an employee receives for the past performance year, bonuses, consideration for promotions, or even disciplinary actions if rated below acceptable levels of performance. The formal performance evaluation form is usually kept in the employee's personnel file as an official company document according to the organization's policies and procedures for record-keeping. You should check with your own human resource department for guidance on your organization's policy.

Informal: day-to-day communication and feedback about performance. Informal feedback is not usually documented; it is rather presented verbally by a supervisor to an employee. The most effective managers ensure they provide this informal, day-to-day feedback and direction to employees. There is no limit on the amount of informal feedback that a supervisor can provide to employees. It could be as frequent as daily. Informal feedback can be positive to reinforce good performance or negative to address any performance issues at the moment. Informal feedback doesn't have to take a lot of time. It can be a passing comment or even a thank you to an employee to recognize completing a job or task. It could also include providing guidance on how to perform a particular task more effectively or correctly.

Which do you think is most important to performance: informal or formal feedback? You actually need both to effectively provide the right amount and type of feedback that employees need to perform their jobs to the best of their ability. A manager's goal should be to provide a balance of both formal and informal feedback to each employee who works for her. Providing only one of these types of feedback at the expense of the other can be a problem. If either formal or informal is not provided to employees, a serious gap could grow in the employee's understanding. Employees want and need to receive both formal and informal feedback. Each should support the other. When a manager provides regular informal feedback to an employee, there will be no surprises at the end of the year, when the formal feedback includes the aggregate of the whole year's performance. Informal feedback should likewise be reciprocal of the formal feedback process, because it reinforces and continues the topics presented during the employee's annual performance review.

Engaged Managing Tips

How a supervisor corrects poor or ineffective performance very often determines just how successful he is in helping that person improve her performance in the future.

FIVE-STEP MANAGING TIPS

1. Observe and assess the specific job performance behavior(s) of an employee.

2. Decide if it is effective or ineffective job performance.

3. If it is effective behavior:

   ● Point out what is effective about the behavior.

   ● Explain why it should be continued and the benefits of doing the job right.

   ● Praise or compliment the employee for this effective behavior, as appropriate.

4. If it is ineffective behavior:

   ● Tell the employee to stop the behavior and explain why it is ineffective.

   ● Explain what an alternative behavior would be and why the alternative behavior would be better.

5. Reinforce the correct behavior when observed in the future.

As a supervisor who corrects poor performance, it is important to not only point out that the employee is doing something wrong, but also to tell why it is wrong, why it is ineffective to do it that way, what the desired performance is, and why it is better to do the right way. When the employee understands why you are asking him to change the performance behavior and why it is important to perform the task correctly, he is more likely to make the change, as well as more likely to trust his manager in the future. The same is true when telling an employee that she is performing a job or task correctly and these same steps should be followed: tell her that she is doing well, and why, and how that fits into the overall workflow. Too often, this explanation is skipped, and the employee doesn't understand why performing the job or task correctly is necessary. Taking the time to point out this important information helps the employee be more engaged.

Recognition

An important part of creating a more engaged workplace is providing recognition to employees. The results of many employee engagement surveys typically show that many employees do not feel they are recognized for their hard work and efforts on the job. Recognizing employees' good performance must be personalized and tailored to each employee's individual needs. The goal of recognition is not only to acknowledge someone for his significant contributions and good work, but also to reinforce these behaviors so they will be repeated in the future. You need to understand what your employees perceive to be reinforcement. That way, what you think is reinforcing to employees actually is doing what you hope to accomplish with your recognition efforts. Sometimes, we think we are reinforcing or rewarding someone, when we are actually doing the opposite. Remember, one person's reward may be another's punishment. For example, you could give someone the chance to speak in front of a large group as recognition, when he is actually petrified of public speaking.

It is important to give some careful thought to the effectiveness of your reward programs and efforts to provide positive reinforcement for employees. Even the best of intentions can have the opposite effect if you get this wrong. Instead of providing a positive recognition experience, you could actually be creating a punishing experience, one that employees would prefer not to repeat. This could counter your efforts to create a more engaged workplace and could reinforce the behaviors you do not want to see continued in the future.

One way to prevent this recognition gone wrong scenario is to ask employees what they would want to receive as recognition. You might be surprised at how inexpensive and easy it may be to provide these types of reinforcement to employees as a reward for their hard work and accomplishments.

 **WIIFM?**

Think about some of the many advantages to your employees dealing with conflict more effectively. Think about the story in this chapter about Hillary Wellington, and how conflict amongst her employees was making her group a dysfunctional team. Remember how she ended up addressing conflict proactively, and how this helped her group work better together as a team.

1. What might be some advantages to dealing directly with any conflicts in your work group or area?

    _____

    _____

    _____

 **Leadership Challenge**

Think about situations in which you as a leader have been faced with conflict amongst the members of your work team or group. Ask yourself the following questions:

1. How has your conflict strategy and style been useful to you on your job?

    _____

    _____

    _____

2. How might you change from a less productive strategy used in the past to a more productive strategy?

_____

_____

_____

3. How can you utilize the *collaborate* conflict strategy more than you do now? How could this help create a more cooperative working environment for everyone involved?

_____

_____

_____

4. Think about a time when you had to deal with an upset employee and how you handled this situation. Looking back, do you think you dealt with this upset employee in the best manner possible? What could you have done differently?

_____

_____

_____

5. What are some opportunities for you to provide more frequent and meaningful feedback to your employees? Do you think that this feedback could help them better perform their jobs? Why do you think this might be the case?

_____

_____

_____

_____

6. How can you ensure that you are recognizing and rewarding your employees in ways that will be most appreciated?

_____

_____

_____

Leader Action Planner

1. What are some of the things you need to do to reduce your own stress in the workplace?

   _____

   _____

   _____

2. How can you get started?

   _____

   _____

   _____

HELP MAKE YOUR WORKPLACE A MORE SATISFYING PLACE TO WORK

It's obvious by now that creating a workplace based on employee engagement creates a better place to work for everyone, including you as the leader. Every process and system in the organization potentially will be improved by the introduction of employee engagement in a workplace. Through employee engagement, everyone who works for a manager will then share in her responsibilities as a leader. With the help of employee engagement, better decisions are possible based on expertise and the input of more people who have a stake in the outcome because they are now involved more directly in these decisions. This can only lead to decisions that are more supported by everyone involved and affected. Think about many potential benefits of creating a more satisfying workplace, such as lower turnover, better qualified new candidates, higher productivity, lower absenteeism, and so on.

Principles of Employee Engagement

There are certain timeless principles about employee engagement which are indisputable and will be true in any work environment. Here are examples of these basic principles about employee engagement:

- Asking employees what they think will give you better, more practical solutions to problems.

- Giving employees greater problem-solving and decision-making ability will engage them more in their jobs and organization.

- Employees do want to do a good job and they get frustrated when they feel they aren't given the opportunity by the organization to perform to their potential.

- Improving communication throughout the organization will help employees become more engaged.

- Providing the right training and development for your employees is a good invest- ment in everyone's future in the organization.

- Equipping your employees with the right tools and resources will improve their productivity.

- Creating a more engaged workplace will reduce employee turnover.

- Your employees have more ability and potential than you may presently realize.

- Employees who follow the rules get upset if they believe others are allowed to break the rules and get away with it.

- Punishing failure will result in less risk-taking and less creativity in the organization in the future.

- Everyone needs to be recognized for their hard work and accomplishments on the job.

- People need feedback to grow and develop on the job.

- Everyone's perception of fairness is different. It is important to try to understand each person's perspective and feelings about how they are treated on the job.

- Money is not the only motivator for employees to do a good job. Intangibles such as recognition, respect, dignity, and growth (to name a few), are also very important to employees.

- Employees do care about the success and future of the organization. They have vested interest in the organization doing well and they want to be involved in achieving this goal, but they must have opportunities to give the company their support.

10 Benefits of Employee Engagement

There are countless benefits to introducing employee engagement into your organization which potentially can be realized by both yourself and those who report to you. The following are just 10 of these potential benefits:

- **Greater job satisfaction:** Both you and your employees will feel a greater sense of job satisfaction. You will feel more like you have the support and cooperation of everyone on your team and there will be less finger-pointing and blaming others. Employees will feel they are valued and that what they have to say is important so they can make a significant contribution.

- **More positive work environment:** Employee engagement creates a work environment in which everyone feels more positive about coming to work. They enjoy working on shared goals and being part of a team. They form stronger working relationships and learn to have more trust in one another as well as in their leadership.

- **Less stressful workplace:** Employee engagement can make work less stressful because employees have greater input and control into decisions and problem solving rather than feeling like they do not have an impact at work. Employees feel less like a victim and more in control of their destiny as an employee. As their leader, you will feel the same way.

- **Cooperation throughout the organization:** Employee engagement teaches everyone that they are on the same team and they should not be competing with one another. Infighting and a lack of cooperation within an organization only benefit the competition: those other organizations who want to take your business away for themselves.

- **Greater trust:** Employee engagement helps create greater trust between employees and their managers by creating better communication. Sharing information demonstrates this trust and helps employees be less suspicious about what is happening in the organization at the higher levels of management.

- **Happier employees:** Happiness is hard to measure, but engaged employees will tell you they are generally happier about their roles in the organization and about their feelings toward their employers. Engaged employees spend less time complaining about the organization and its leaders and invest more of their emotional energy into doing a better job.

- **Personal growth:** Employee engagement can unlock the potential of employees. Bringing out their talents and abilities by providing opportunities at work to use these skills—in ways that may never have been possible in a more traditionally managed organizational culture—expands your people and your organization.

- **Teamwork:** Employee engagement encourages stronger teamwork by providing more opportunities for employees to work together to reach shared goals rather than only individual goals.

- **Employee loyalty:** Loyalty works both ways: You have to be loyal to get loyalty back. Engaged employees have a stronger sense of loyalty for their employer because they feel that the organization cares about them and respects their abilities as employees.

- **Customer satisfaction:** There is an old saying in business which advises "If you want your employees to treat your customers better, then treat your employees well." This advice certainly applies to employee engagement. If you want your employees to focus on the needs of your customers, then you need to focus on the needs of your employees. Engaged employees will be far more concerned about meeting or exceeding the needs of your customers than if they were disgruntled or disengaged in their jobs. Engaged employees put forth that discretionary effort, which can make all the difference in the world when it comes to customer satisfaction, regardless of the employee's position or role in the organization.

Accept the Leadership Engagement Challenge

There are many misconceptions about employee engagement, but the bottom line is: Employee engagement is all about leadership. Engagement not only makes the workplace a better and more fulfilling experience for employees, but for leaders as well. It is much more satisfying to lead employees who are committed and interested in their work, compared to employees who need help just getting their jobs done. For you, it could be easier to meet your objectives as a manager if those who work for you are more motivated to help reach those objectives. Imagine what it might be like to have everyone fully engaged in their jobs and to have fully contributing members of your team.

Creating a workplace based on employee engagement is not just something nice to do; it can produce remarkable results. Learning to become a more engaging leader can not only help you as a manager become a more effective leader today, but can also help you reach your future career goals.

 **WIIFM?**

1. Think about all of the potential advantages discussed throughout this book that employee engagement can create for you in your leadership position. What would be your top five?

   _____

   _____

   _____

   _____

   _____

2. What do you need to do to take advantage of employee engagement?

   _____

   _____

   _____

   _____

   _____

APPENDIX

The following *Employee Engagement Survey* is designed to correspond to each of the chapters in this book. Each of the 10 questions relates to the subject matter presented in the corresponding chapter of this book. Ask your employees to complete this brief survey. It will give you a better understanding of which areas of your supervisor leadership skills are strongest and which need improvement concerning employee engagement in your work group. The survey can be copied and provided to your employees to complete.

Employee Engagement Survey

1. I feel like I am encouraged to contribute my thoughts and opinions at work by my supervisor.

1	2	3	4	5
Disagree		Neutral		Strongly Agree

2. I believe that my job would be more interesting if I were given additional responsibilities and given the opportunity to make more decisions concerning my work.

1	2	3	4	5
Disagree		Neutral		Strongly Agree

3. I receive information about how the work I perform is important to the organization's success and goals.

1	2	3	4	5
Disagree		Neutral		Strongly Agree

4. I feel like I have good working relationships with co-workers and my supervisor, and having these good relationships helps me perform my job better.

1	2	3	4	5
Disagree		Neutral		Strongly Agree

5. I feel that I am committed to doing a good job based on my working relationship with others, especially my manager.

1	2	3	4	5
Disagree		Neutral		Strongly Agree

6. I believe that my job skills could be improved if I were given the opportunity to become more involved in the problem-solving and decision-making process at work.

1	2	3	4	5
Disagree		Neutral		Strongly Agree

7. I feel that I am given the opportunity to provide suggestions and solve problems at work which I believe could be a benefit to the organization.

1	2	3	4	5
Disagree		Neutral		Strongly Agree

8. I feel that I receive enough information to be able to perform my job as expected.

1	2	3	4	5
Disagree		Neutral		Strongly Agree

9. I feel in control of most of the variables that directly affect my ability to do my job at a level that I would like to be able to perform.

1	2	3	4	5
Disagree		Neutral		Strongly Agree

10. I am basically satisfied with my job and my role in the organization.

1	2	3	4	5
Disagree		Neutral		Strongly Agree

Interpreting the Survey Results

Which questions did your employees score lowest on from this survey? You need to focus on these areas the most to increase the level of employee engagement in your organization. Look back at the corresponding chapters for each question, and reread this information and advice to address these issues. Similarly, look at the questions on the survey that you received the highest scores on, and look at the corresponding chapters related to these questions to see how you can continue to improve the level of engagement in your work group and organization. Since your employees need to learn from positive and negative feedback, so do you.

ABOUT THE AUTHOR

 **Peter R. Garber** is the author of more than 50 books and training products on a wide variety of human resources and business topics. *The Manager's Employee Engagement Toolbox* is his third title published by ASTD Press. Mr. Garber has worked as a human resource professional for more than 33 years. He has also been an adjunct faculty member at the University of Pittsburgh, where he taught leadership courses using many of the concepts presented in this latest book. Mr. Garber and his wife currently reside in Los Angeles, California.

INDEX